CARPE DIEM

CARPE DIEM

PUT A LITTLE LATIN IN YOUR LIFE

Harry Mount

HYPERION

NEW YORK

The Browning Version © Trustees of the Terence Ratigan Trust 1953.
Reprinted by permission of the publisher: www.nickhernbooks.com.

Copyright © 2007 Harry Mount

Printed in the United States of America. For information address Hyperion,
77 West 66th Street, New York, New York 10023-6298.

Library of Congress Cataloging-in-Publication Data
Mount, Harry
[Amo, amas, amat—and all that]
Carpe diem : put a little Latin in your life / Harry Mount.
p.   cm.
Originally published: Amo, amas, amat—and all that. London : Short, 2006.
ISBN 978-1-4013-2234-2
1. Latin language—Grammar—Problems, exercises, etc.   2. Latin
language—Humor. I. Title.
PA2087.5.M68   2007
478.82'421—dc22   2007012732

Hyperion books are available for special promotions, premiums,
or corporate training. For details contact Michael Rentas, Proprietary Markets,
Hyperion, 77 West 66th Street, 12th floor, New York,
New York 10023, or call 212-456-0133.

Design by Cathryn S. Aison

FIRST EDITION

1   3   5   7   9   10   8   6   4   2

For William and Mary

Mons Maximus et Mons Maxima

CONTENTS

CONTENTS

The study of the Classics teaches us to believe that there is something really great and excellent in the world, surviving all the shocks of accident and fluctuations of opinion, and raises us above that low and servile fear which bows only to present power and upstart authority.

William Hazlitt, *The Round Table* (1817)

Classics—from the Latin "*classicus, -a, -um,*" meaning "of the highest class."

The New Oxford Dictionary of English (2001)

CARPE DIEM

INTRODUCTION

A ngelina Jolie did not study Latin at the Lee Strasberg Theater Institute in Los Angeles, which she attended from the age of eleven in the mid-'80s. Nor did the subject crop up at NYU where she went on to do film studies. But all the same, when she was photographed passing through London's Heathrow Airport on January 25, 2006, on the way to the economic summit at Davos, the tattoo she revealed on the lower slopes of her pregnant belly was in Latin.

"*Quod me nutrit me destruit*," read the tattoo—"What nourishes me destroys me." I also notice that Miss Jolie has decided to change the name of her newly adopted, three-year-old Vietnamese son, Pham Quang Sang, to Pax Thien Jolie (*Pax, pacis f.*—peace).

David Beckham, the English soccer player who has just started playing with the Los Angeles Galaxy, shares her tastes. He, too, was no Latin scholar at Chingford School in Essex, England, when he was there in the late 1980s. But still, when it comes to his body art, the soccer star is a dedicated Latinist. Of the nine tattoos on his body, three are in Latin (and two of the others, "Victoria" and "Romeo," are Latin-inspired names).

On his left forearm, he has the tricky little expression "*Ut Amem et Foveam*"—"That I might love and cherish"—which makes careful and correct use of the subjunctive.

On his right forearm, he has the number of the soccer shirt he wears—7—although he opts for the Roman numeral, VII. Under the VII, Beckham has had his Manchester tattooist, Louis Malloy, retained since the soccer player's days at Manchester United, write "*Perfectio in Spiritu*"—"Perfection in Spirit."

Why do these stars, with no formal knowledge of the language, go crazy for it?

As Miss Jolie is no doubt aware, the Latin on her tummy and in her son's new name has echoes resonating back through the ages and through the pens of the greatest writers of all time. That's why she has the quote and name in Latin, and not in English or Swahili; for the same reason, she had it printed in a Gothic font—to give an impression of ancient wisdom.

The same desire for something old and highbrow means that the former French president, Jacques Chirac, wanted to call his new European Internet search engine (if it comes off)

When it comes to body art, David Beckham

is a dedicated Latinist

"*Quaero*"—meaning "I seek" in Latin—rather than "*Je cherche*."

Latin's ancient grandeur has appealed for centuries to people who want to come across as a little bit special. Because the study of classics had no practical use, it tended to gain cachet among those who could afford to dedicate their time to fine prose, poetry, and history rather than to money-making disciplines such as science or engineering. It flourished in American Catholic and prep schools, and in Britain's public and grammar schools—and today proper teaching of it only really survives in these privileged little pockets.

Although Angelina Jolie and David Beckham may not be aware of the history of Latin in the American and British education systems, they will be aware of the inherited baggage of poshness that comes with the language. For the same reason, the organizers of the Superbowl are careful to call it Superbowl XLI and not Superbowl 41. Arabic numerals just don't have the same cachet—and that has nothing to do with al-Qa'eda.

Miss Jolie will have noticed the chunk of Latin associated with the MGM studio—"*Ars gratia artis*," "Art for the sake of art"—which is seen above the roaring lion at the opening of all their films. Beckham will have picked up on the Latin in the mottos of soccer clubs (the motto of one of the great English soccer teams, Arsenal, is "*Victoria Concordia Crescit*"—not "Posh Spice goes by Concorde," but "Victory grows through togetherness"). Beckham might have noticed, too, the classical influence behind the grouped Ionic columns that frame the

pedimented porch of his mock–Queen Anne house, Becking-
ham Palace in Sawbridgeworth, Hertfordshire. Jolie and Beckham will have seen Latin, too, in dates on war memorials and
in epitaphs on tombstones, and carved as inscriptions on the
facades of ancient houses. Wherever Angelina Jolie and Beckham will have spotted Latin, its setting will have been grand,
or attached to the portentous things in life: birth, death, scholarship boards. The setting will also have tended to be an old
one, or one that wants to conjure up connotations of oldness.

The knowledge that Latin has survived in written, if not
in spoken, form for 2,500 years gives *"Quod me nutrit me destruit"* an elemental force that just isn't there in "What nourishes me destroys me." Angelina Jolie may not be able to read
Latin, but she will recognize it when she hears it in everyday
speech: RIP (*requiescat in pace*); i.e. (*id est*—that is); and so on.

All of these terms are mental triggers, little tics—dotted
through the English language and cropping up in solid form all
over Britain and America—that give Latin what Angelina
Jolie's agent would call tremendous branding potential.

And so to the point of this book: to make the jump from
a Hollywood tattooist's knowledge of Latin to a level where
you can understand most of those inscriptions on tombstones,
and get real pleasure from reading bits of Horace and Catullus,
is not difficult.

If you never learned Latin at school—no matter. If you
did, all the better. You might think you've forgotten it. You
haven't. If you spent even the tiniest part of your teenage years
learning dreary declensions and conjugations, the effort made

to do so, and the young age at which you did it, means that a ghost of that knowledge is still there, tattooed to the back of your brain. Somewhere in your mind there still beat the old rhythms—*amo, amas, amat*; ablative absolutes; the future perfect; subjunctives.

As you go down the list, and the rules behind each idiom get a little more complicated, they may grow a little more faded; but all those rules need is a little memory boost, and they come flooding back. It will only take a quick trawl through this friendly Latin primer, with its reminders of a few of those declensions and conjugations, to bring the ghost to life. The joy that a little learning of Latin brings is immense.

Alexander Pope was quite wrong, by the way, when he said, "A little learning is a dangerous thing, drink deep or taste not the Pierian spring."

His miscalculation is particularly disappointing in somebody who certainly knew his classics, and would have known that Pieria was the place where, according to Hesiod, the Nine Muses were born—Clio, in charge of history; Urania, astronomy; Calliope, epic poetry; Melpomene, tragedies; Euterpe, harmony; Erato, lyric and love poetry; Terpsichore, dancing; Thalia, comedy; and Polyhymnia, music. All of these Muses are delightful subjects, of which a little knowledge can bring vast pleasure.

Okay, I do have to admit the Muses were Greek, like an awful lot of things absorbed by the Romans: tragedy, comedy, architecture; so many things in fact that Quintilian said with some relief, "*Satura quidem tota nostra est*"—"At least satire is completely ours."

But leave the Greek influences on Rome up to me. Wherever they are essential to our understanding, I will tie them in.

As for the power and beauty of Latin, this is perhaps best caught in the story of an English botanist on holiday in Rome a few springs ago. On a tour of the Colosseum (*colosseus, -a, -um*—colossal), the botanist saw a flower he'd never seen in Italy before. Puzzled, he started to look closely at the other flowers growing between the flagstones in the old arena (from *harena, -ae, f.*—sand; i.e., the sand that was sprinkled in front of the *auditorium, -i, n.*—a place of audience) and the cracks in the stone seats of the terraces. The flowers weren't native to Rome, or even to Italy. The bemused botanist left the Colosseum to go and look at the patches of grass nearby— under the Arch of Titus, over the Capitoline Hill, and in the stadium (*stadium, -i, n.*—a running track). He couldn't find a trace of these exotic flowers outside the arena at all.

When he took the flowers back to his Cambridge labora- tory, he found that they had come from precise, verifiable places: Libya and Tunisia mostly. The only feasible explana- tion he could come up with was that the flowers had grown from seeds that had lodged in the coats of lions brought from Africa to eat Roman prisoners in the Colosseum 2,000 years before. The seeds must have fallen off as the lions got stuck into some serious fighting with their Christian victims.

This story is a neat analogy for the evolution of Latin— an ancient language that traveled across the world, had seem- ingly died, and yet still blossoms today in the oddest of places.

Never mind the fact that most of the people who now come across the flowers of Latin haven't the faintest idea that those flowers have their roots in that language. Architecture, Roman numerals, satire, comedy, the right use of particular words . . . Once you can link up the modern incarnation with its Latin root, the rewards are thrilling.

In his Booker Prize–winning novel, *The Line of Beauty*, Alan Hollinghurst described those people who know all the big turning points in history as being able to look back at the world as an enfilade of rooms: Greece gives way to Rome . . . Rome to the Byzantine Empire . . . the Renaissance . . . the British Empire . . . America . . . and so on.

Knowing a bit of Latin is an invitation to the biggest room in the building, with a view down the corridor to all the succeeding ages. And you can get your hands on that invitation at any age. Alfred the Great, who knew how crucial it was to learn Latin to become a civilized man, took it up in his thirties.

PROSECCO AND PISTACHIO—OR
HOW TO READ THIS BOOK

M y favorite guidebook is called *Venice for Pleasure*, by J. G. Links. That is exactly what it does—shows you all the pleasure of Venice without any of the "Oh, God, I ought to go to the Accademia at some stage and hoist in four million Tintorettos; but, Christ, I'd prefer a pistachio ice cream and a glass of prosecco."

J. G. Links's plan was not to show you the ice creams and proseccos (*siccus, -a, -um, adj.*—dry). He said you could find a café yourself; there are plenty of perfectly good ones all over Venice. The same went for the four million Tintorettos: you could get a highbrow *Fodor's* yourself, full of dates and architectural glossaries. His plan instead was to take you for a lovely walk around the highlights and obscure golden corners of

Venice, leaving you to do all the Tintorettos if and when you felt mentally strong enough.

Well, that's sort of the plan in this book. It would be vain to say that reading it will be as pleasant as walking round St. Mark's Square after a pistachio ice cream and three glasses of prosecco. Lovely as Latin is, learning it is not all pleasure.

The expert on the tricky bits of Latin is Nigel Molesworth. Molesworth is the heroically lazy schoolboy hero of the comic classics by Geoffrey Willans and Ronald Searle, which told the tale of an old-fashioned British prep school in the 1950s. "Actually, it is quite easy to be topp (sic) in lat. you just have to work," said Molesworth.

The point of this book is to make learning Latin as pleasurable as possible, allowing you to gently pick up (cf. Kirk, Captain—"to boldly go where no man has gone before," why split infinitives are okay, *infra*, see below) the rudiments without feeling like an eleven-year-old faced with a long summer evening full of conjugations and declensions to memorize all over again.

All that daunting stuff is here: principal parts, locatives, ablative absolutes. And you can sit down and learn it all on long summer evenings if you want. But I've tried to make this a book you can read straight through, with the conjugations and declensions, etc. (*et cetera*—and the rest), sectioned off in boxes to be learned as you come across them, or later, or not at all.

Although I've used all those nightmarish expressions like conditional clauses and subjunctives, I've also called them things like "woulda/shoulda/coulda" words. Call it dumbing down if you like. If you think you're clever, just convert these patronizing expressions back into conditional clauses and subjunctives or whatever. If you're happy being dumb, stick to the easy expressions.

I've also included some little chunks on Roman architecture and literature, but they really are little. There simply wasn't room here to do justice to Roman roads, underfloor heating, and the Romans' million other contributions to modern civilization.

Throughout the book, I have dropped in bits of vocabulary, marked VOCAB. In a slightly irritating way, to drum things in, I've also put in brackets the Latin derivation (*derivo, -are*— I derive) of certain words and explained Latin idioms that have crept into the language unexplained, i.e., when I write "*i.e.*" I'll put (*id est*—that is) after it, when I use it for the first time.

But you don't have to work that hard. This book doesn't have all the declensions and conjugations that you'll ever need; for that you can go to the Latin equivalent of *Fodor's*, *Kennedy's Latin Primer.*

EATING SHORTBREAD ON THE BANKS OF LAKE GENEVA

My father likes to tell the story of the great fortunes made by the writers of Latin and Greek grammar books. There may never have been that many people doing Latin or Greek at any one particular time, but every one of them needed a Lewis and Short dictionary and a *Kennedy's Shorter Latin Primer*. The *Primer* was the *vademecum* (literally "go with me"—a crucial book you take everywhere with you) of the Latin-learning boy. And it was normally boys; it's still the case that more boys than girls tend to learn Latin and at an earlier age.

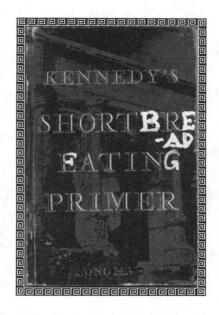

The book of books, written by the Shrewsbury
headmaster Benjamin Hall Kennedy in 1875,
revised by Sir James Mountford, Liverpool
University's Professor of Latin, in 1930, and
customized by me, aged ten

With its distinctive psychedelic, bleached-blue cover picture of the Colosseum and its ancient-looking font—as if a Roman sculptor had just finished carving it into a tablet—the *Primer* was a popular target for graffiti. With a few deft Sharpie strokes, it was quickly transformed by a million schoolboys into *Kennedy's Shortbread Eating Primer.* Boys bought multiple copies because primers got so heavily mutilated, and were often stolen because they were so vital.

Anyway, so my father's story goes, the money made by the schoolmasters every year out of a fresh generation of eight-year-olds, and a staler generation of nine-year-old graffiti artists who had to replace their copies, was so vast that the masters decamped en masse to live in tax exile in vast, deep-eaved chalets by Lake Geneva.

If you took a walk by a Swiss lake in the 1930s—the peak time for the writing of Latin grammar books—you could hardly fail to bump into knots of bespectacled millionaires swapping gags about ablative absolutes and rogue gerundives. Here, footling around in a rowing boat in the shallows of Lake Geneva, was Benjamin Hall Kennedy, the original writer of the *Primer*, in deep conversation over cognate accusatives with the man who revised it in 1930, Sir James Mountford. There was Liddell, deep in conversation over a glühwein with Scott about the correct Greek word for the most terrible of Athenian punishments—"to stuff a radish up the fundament" (*raphanidosis,* by the way).

Even if my father's story exaggerates the takings for classics grammar books, it does uphold one basic truth: that those books have been in print for seventy years or more, a lot longer than plenty of books about living languages.

In 2004, *Kennedy's Latin Primer* entered its seventy-eighth impression, and that was just of Sir James Mountford's 1962 edition. The original B. H. Kennedy edition went through dozens of further impressions. And the reason why they went through so many is that everything is there: every conjugation, declension, locative, and correlative pronoun. There was no need for a new book.

So, as J. G. Links says in his guidebook, by all means keep a copy of the dry masterpieces to hand—in his case, the *Fodor's*; in our case, the *Primer*.

The idea here is rather to give you a pleasurable breeze through the main principles of Latin without bringing on the blood, sweat, and tears. Take in what follows and you should be able to negotiate all Latin sentences. This book has the crucial declensions and conjugations you need to know to build a skeleton of Latin knowledge on which Kennedy can fit the flesh.

The two books should complement each other, and if they do, and popular success follows, and little boys find it within their hearts to mutilate this book, I hope there's still space beside the shores of Lake Geneva to squeeze in another chalet.

In brief, if you already know the bare bones of Latin, by the time you've finished this book, your dormant knowledge (*dormio, dormire*—I sleep) will have woken up.

And, if you have no knowledge, dormant or otherwise,

The inscription on Bruni's tomb
in Santa Croce, Florence

you'll have the basics, which should mean you'll at least be able to translate this, the simple Latin—but all the more moving for that—of Leonardo Bruni's epitaph in the church of Santa Croce in Florence. Bruni, by the way, was an eminent Florentine humanist and classicist (1369–1444), best known for his Latin history of Florence, *Historiarum Florentinarum Libri XII.*

> *Postquam Leonardus e vita migravit*
> *Historia luget; eloquentia muta est*

Ferturque musas tum Graecas tum
Latinas lacrimas tenere non potuisse.

The translation is given on the last page of this book. Don't cheat by looking now.

BACK TO BASICS—SEX, CASES, AND WORD ORDER

❧❧❧❧❧

How we laughed in 1981 when we were ten and learning Latin for the first time in 4 Pi, my class in my prep school, North Bridge House in London's Regent's Park. How silly it seemed that Romans actually talked the stuff we were learning, like the Romans did in the French cartoon strip *Asterix*—about the plucky villagers in ancient Gaul who took on the Italian invaders. Lovely, patient, and gentle as our Latin teacher, Mrs. Pickersgill—Marilyn Monroe meets Miss Jean Brodie—was, Latin seemed by contrast such a precise, concise, rigid language.

And it didn't help that all the Romans seemed to talk about were *fossae* and *valla*, ditches and ramparts, and *sagittae* and *bella*, arrows and wars. We also had to learn so many declensions, conjugations, and rules that it seemed extra-ordinary that you could ever master them well enough to have an easygoing chat about Ben Hur's chances in the Rome Derby, or whether Livia was really having an affair with Germanicus. And how on earth did they always remember what the verb in their sentences was and save it till the end?

One joke our little minds found particularly funny was to take everyday English conversations—"Morning, how are you?"—and turn them into stiff, fossilized Latin.

One friend of mine took the joke even further by talking Latin in a slangy, easygoing way. "*Sat est,*" he would say when he was annoyed; short for "*Satis est*"—"That's enough."

Julian Morrow, the dedicated veteran tutor in Donna Tartt's best-selling novel, *The Secret History* (1992), played the same game with his star pupil, Henry Winter.

Julian and he were talking—in jocular, mocking, pedantic Latin—like a couple of priests tidying the vestry before a mass. A dark smell of brewing tea hung strong in the air.

Henry glanced up.

"*Salve, amice* [Hello, pal]," he said, and a subtle animation flickered in his rigid features, usually so locked up and distant. "*Valesne? Quid est rei?* [How are you? What's up?]"

"You look well," I said to him, and he did.

He inclined his head slightly. His eyes, which had

been murky and dilated while he was ill, were now the clearest of blues.

"*Benigne dicis* [You speak kindly/How nice of you to say so]," he said, "I feel much better."

On reflection, the reason Latin seemed such a strange language to chat in was not so much because of its strangeness but because it was dead. You can imagine people speaking much odder languages, like Finnish—which, like Estonian and Hungarian, is one of the few languages in Europe that doesn't share the Indo-European roots common to, among others, Latin, English, French, Frisian, Russian, Bengali, Hindi, and Farsi. That's presumably because there are still lots of living Finns around, speaking Finnish.

Latin, though, died before the age of recording—most surviving instances of it, apart from the cod Latin spoken in the Vatican and dialects surviving in the odd Swiss canton, are formal, preserved in deeply thought-out poetry, prose, and documents. And yet of course it was a language that people once used to talk about the weather and their sex lives; people laughed and cried in Latin. The modern language that gives us the best example of what spoken Latin was like is Italian. Yes, that most hot-blooded, passionate, and angry of languages is only a small jump from Latin.

English, on the other hand, is a bloody big jump from Latin. They are such different languages that a literal translation from one to the other sounds and looks very awkward, like putting a big foot in a small sock. English is not nearly as close a relative of Latin as French, and even French is a descendant through many generations. Kingsley Amis shows what a great chasm there is between Latin and French in an imaginary dialogue "between a scrounging legionary, perhaps a Vandal or a Parthian by origin, and a willing but benighted yokel [in ancient Gaul, which became France]":

> LEGIONARY: (in vile Latin): I want water. Bring me water. Aquam.
> YOKEL: Ugh?
> LEGIONARY: Aquam! Say aquam, you bloody fool. Go on—aquam.
> YOKEL: O? [To be spelled "eau" when they get to the writing stage centuries later.]
> LEGIONARY: Bring it to the high cliff. The high cliff. Altum.
> YOKEL: Ugh?
> LEGIONARY: Altum! Say altum, you bumpkin. Go on—altum.
> YOKEL: O? [To be spelled "haut" when etc.]

The English jump is a bigger stretch.

> LEGIONARY: Our chaps are thinking of calling this place Eboracum. Go on, say it, you bog-trotter.
> YOKEL: York?

Kingsley Amis on Latin
[*The King's English: A Guide to Modern Usage*, 1997]

It may be worth looking at how the English language developed, once the Romans left Britain to be conquered by the Angles and Saxons.

The language they brought with them, Anglo-Saxon, itself borrowed lots of words from Latin, either directly or via French. And then, when the Normans came, their brand of French imported even more Latinate words. Indeed over the centuries English was mutilated and diluted by so many different languages that its incorporation of Latin was random and chaotic.

So, to say you need to understand Latin to understand English, as some people do say, is as crazy as suggesting that you need to understand Anglo-Saxon, German, and Norman French to understand English. Knowing all those languages would certainly be helpful, but it's a bit much to ask.

The *really* useful thing about Latin is not so much that it will help you understand English as that it will help you understand Latin, in which some of the most stirring prose and poetry ever was written. Know Latin, and you will know world literature from the third century BC, when writers got going in Rome, through the so-called Golden Age of Latin: Lucretius, Catullus, Sallust, Cicero, and Caesar; the Augustan Age: Ovid, Horace, Virgil, and Livy; down to the end of the Silver Age in AD 120: Martial, Juvenal, Lucan, Seneca, Pliny, and Tacitus.

The only reason you will know English better as a result of reading Latin is because it is so different from Latin, not because of any similarities. It is in computing the changes from one language to another that you are forced to think about the structure of each of them.

It is also important to remember when writing Latin and translating it, that though dead now and often preserved in stiff forms, it was once as malleable as English, and that it developed enormously in the 1,500 years that it was in use. So do not treat it as a relic to be worshiped, as something to be translated word for word, or, if you're pompous, something to show off about; treat it rather as a way of reading, translating, and writing beautiful and moving prose and poetry.

Before you start producing your free-flowing, honeyed words, though, you've got to know your way round some of the rigid-seeming oddities of Latin. And the first of these oddities is Latin word order.

I YOU LOVE — LATIN WORD ORDER

We put our verbs in the middle of our sentences—"I send batches of flowers hourly to Cameron Diaz." The Romans like to put the verb at the end, as in: "I batches of flowers to Cameron Diaz hourly send." So the traditional Latin word order is Subject Object Verb, or SOV if you want a not particularly inspirational mnemonic.

SOV is a pretty good rule of thumb, but you can play around with it, as lots of Romans, and especially poets, did. Virgil wrote his own epitaph for his tomb in Naples and went wild with his word order:

Mantua me genuit; Calabri rapuere; tenet nunc
Parthenope; cecini pascua, rura, duces.

Mantua gave birth to me; The Calabrians took me
away; now Naples [or Parthenope, its anthropomor-
phic name, from the Greek for "maiden face"] holds
me; I sang of fields, farms, and leaders.

Even though you won't necessarily be able to translate this yet,
you can see that the subject jumps around in each clause.
Mantua and *Calabri* are in the traditional position, at the beginning of the clause. *Parthenope* is at the end, while *cecini*, the
verb—"I sang," is at the beginning of its clause, English-style.
I'd say stick to the SOV rules but just be aware that they can
be played around with.

SEX IN ANCIENT ROME

The three Latin sexes or, better, genders are masculine, feminine, and neuter. We have the same ones—he, she, and it. The
difference is that practically all our nouns are neuter. We call a
cucumber "it" and a soul "it," where the Romans considered
cucumbers (*cucumis, -eris*) masculine and souls (*anima, -ae*)
feminine.

The Latin approach to these things is not as annoying as it
might at first seem. It soon becomes second nature that
words that end in *-us* (like *dominus* and *Augustus*) are masculine;

-*a* words (like *mensa, Diana,* and *Camilla*) are feminine; and -*um* words (like *bellum, pilum, castrum*) are neuter, with a few exceptions that don't have this nice and easy pattern to them.

The other thing that becomes second nature is that adjectives should agree with nouns, i.e., masculine nouns take masculine adjectives, feminine nouns, feminine adjectives, etc. Plural nouns also take plural adjectives. This can provide comfortable room for showing off in English; e.g., the plural of *persona non grata*—an unwelcome person—is *personae non gratae.*

The neuter adjective is a wonderfully pliable thing. On its own, it can be used to mean an object with the qualities of that adjective. So *nigrum* means "black," but it also means "a black thing." That "thing" is itself fairly pliable and can be twisted to mean "circumstance." As a result, *in extremis* literally means "in extreme things," but it also means "in extreme circumstances" and ended up being popularly used to mean "on the verge of death."

THE CASES—OR CHURCHILL'S PROBLEMS WITH A TABLE

Now that you've worked out Latin word order, it's time to deal with the cases that each of those words—subject, object, and the rest of them—go into. There are six cases in Latin. Here they are with their role attached:

> Nominative—The case that the subject in a sentence takes.

Vocative—The case of the person or thing that is addressed.

Accusative—The case that the object of the verb takes.

Genitive—The case that signifies possession. When something belongs to someone, that someone is in the genitive, their position usually signified by the word "of." So in "the Bride of Frankenstein," "Frankenstein" goes in the genitive; in "the girl of my best friend," "my best friend" goes in the genitive; in "the *plume de ma tante*," "*ma tante*" goes in the genitive.

Dative—When something is done "to" or "for" someone or something, that person or thing goes in the dative: "Everything I do, I do it *for* you" (Bryan Adams, 1991).

Ablative—When something is done "by," "with," or "from" someone or something, the person or thing is in the ablative: "By God's grace ["grace" in the ablative], with the right rubbing alcohol ["rubbing alcohol" in the ablative], from any decent ironmonger's ["decent ironmonger" in the ablative], I shall be drunk by dusk."

Here are all the cases, embedded in Hamlet's speech to Rosencrantz about how miserable he is:

"I [the subject, in the nominative] have of late—but wherefore I know not, Rosencrantz [person you're talking to, in the vocative]—lost all my mirth [the object of the verb, in the accusative], forgone all custom of exercises; and indeed it goes so heavily with my disposition that this goodly frame, the earth, seems to me [anything "to" or "for," in the dative] a sterile promontory, this most excellent canopy, the air, look you, this brave o'erhanging firmament, this majestical roof fretted with golden fire [anything "by," "with," or "from"—in the ablative], why, it appears no other thing to me than a foul and pestilent congregation of vapors [anything "of," in the genitive]."

(By the way, I added in the "Rosencrantz" to get a vocative.)

Now that you have got the meaning behind the six cases, you need to know how to form them, hence the First Declension, using the noun *mensa, mensae, f.*—table.

	Singular	**Plural**
NOM.	mensa	mensae
VOC.	mensa	mensae
ACC.	mensam	mensas
GEN.	mensae	mensarum
DAT.	mensae	mensis
ABL.	mensa	mensis

The First Declension: always ends in -a, mostly feminine

The mere mention of the words *mensa, mensa, mensam* . . . will bring on the sweats in some people. God, the hours spent learning all those lists. And, Christ, the pointlessness!

That's certainly what Winston Churchill thought when he was learning Latin at Harrow in the late 1880s.

The method of teaching Latin at Harrow was the same then, as now: rote learning of tables; in this case, literally. Churchill was asked by his Latin master to decline *mensa*, meaning "table." Churchill was confused as to how it was possible that the same form, *mensa*, could be used in three different ways: why it was the same in the nominative, vocative, and ablative.

Here he describes the incident in his autobiography:

"Then why does mensa [in the vocative] also mean 'O table'?" I inquired, "and what does 'O table' mean?"

"Mensa, 'O table,' is the vocative case," the master replied.

"But why 'O table'?" I persisted in genuine curiosity.

"'O table'—you would use that in addressing a table, in invoking a table."

And then seeing that he was not carrying me with him: "You would use it in speaking to a table."

"But I never do," I blurted out in honest amazement.

"If you are impertinent, you will be punished and

punished, let me tell you, very severely," was his con-clusive rejoinder.

Winston Spencer Churchill,
My Early Life (1930)

Churchill had a point. You'd never address a table, ex-cept perhaps to swear at it, when you stub your toe. And, even then, you'd use it in conjunction with a swear word (*Sanguinea mensa*—Bloody table). Nevertheless, all nouns have a voca-tive, inanimate or not.

The consoling thing is that, except for when you're ad-dressing people, you'll hardly ever come across the vocative. The other consoling thing is that the vocative is practically al-ways exactly the same as the nominative, so it's hardly worth learning it.

Annoyingly, we're now going to come across one of the few exceptions to this rule—Second Declension nouns—where the vocative, ending in *-e*, is different to the nomina-tive. There are two types of Second Declension masculine nouns—those ending in *-us* and those ending in *-er*. The *-us* nouns go like *dominus*. The *-er* nouns go like *magister*—master.

	Singular	**Plural**
NOM.	dominus	domini
VOC.	domine	domini
ACC.	dominum	dominos
GEN.	domini	dominorum
DAT.	domino	dominis
ABL.	domino	dominis

The Second Declension: ending in -us

	Singular	**Plural**
NOM.	magister	magistri
VOC.	magister	magistri
ACC.	magistrum	magistros
GEN.	magistri	magistrorum
DAT.	magistro	magistris
ABL.	magistro	magistris

The Second Declension: ending in -er

The name of the game dominoes is obscurely derived from *dominus*, meaning master. The hoods worn in 1710 by Italian priests—grand figures, considered a type of master—were called dominoes. Black with holes cut into them for the eyes, their name got passed on to the black rectangular playing blocks with their white dots.

This connection between *dominus* and dominoes wouldn't immediately spring to the mind of even the greatest Latinist; I've just had to look it up.

The distance between the two words is enough to show that a knowledge of Latin doesn't necessarily unlock the secret of lots of obscure Latinate words.

In fact, it's a good idea to try to avoid Latinate words when translating Latin. This isn't just because Latin words don't always translate into similar-sounding Latinate English words. It's also that, for all the beauty of Latin, Latinate words in English are often clumsy and pompous, as you should find out in the next chapter.

GEORGE ORWELL, BERKS, AND WANKERS—OR HOW TO TRANSLATE LATIN INTO LOVELY ENGLISH

🎹🎹🎹🎹🎹

When it comes to translating Latin into English, the real joy comes in doing what Latin teacher after Latin teacher begged you to do—"Be more imaginative, Mount. Who's ever said, 'Sejanus, needing to be promoted, enjoined the centurions to go by, with, or from home'? Much better to say, 'Sejanus was so desperate to curry favor with the emperor that he ordered all the centurions to quit the city by nightfall or he'd have their eyeballs skewered on the Traitors' Gate of Tiberius's palace at dawn.'"

Here is Orwell, on the potential pitfalls of translation:

> Bad writers, and especially scientific, political, and sociological writers, are nearly always haunted by the

notion that Latin or Greek words are grander than Saxon ones, and unnecessary words like expedite, ameliorate, predict, extraneous, deracinated, clandestine, subaqueous, and hundreds of others constantly gain ground from their Anglo-Saxon numbers.

The jargon peculiar to Marxist writing (hyena, hangman, cannibal, petty bourgeois, gentry, lackey, flunkey, mad dog, White Guard, etc.) consists largely of words translated from Russian, German, or French; but the normal way of coining a new word is to use a Latin or Greek root with the appropriate affix and, where necessary, the size formation. It is often easier to make up words of this kind (deregionalize, impermissible, extramarital, non-fragmentary, and so forth) than to think up the English words that will cover one's meaning. The result, in general, is an increase in slovenliness and vagueness . . . The inflated style itself is a kind of euphemism. A mass of Latin words falls upon the facts like soft snow, blurring the outline and covering up all the details.

George Orwell,
Politics and the English Language (1946)

This doesn't mean that, as Orwell elsewhere acknowledges, good writing is simply a matter of having as few Latinate words as possible, and exchanging them for Anglo-Saxon ones. Sometimes, particularly with new and scientific words, the Latinate word is the only choice. You might even want that extra touch of pomposity and archness that the Latinate words brings.

But on the whole Orwell was right. A too-literal use of Latin leads to a constipated use of English.

Kingsley Amis debates the danger of this constipated English in his last, posthumously published, book, *The King's English: A Guide to Modern Usage* (1997), where he divides English language pedants into Berks and Wankers. Berk is almost an affectionate insult. Although it comes from Cockney rhyming slang (Berkshire Hunt rhymes with ****), Berk really means some kind of confident nerd. Wanker is more aggressive. Anyway, here are Kingsley Amis's definitions of the words when applied to the use of English:

> BERKS are careless, coarse, crass, gross and of what anybody would agree is a lower social class than one's own. They speak in a slipshod way with dropped Hs, intruded glottal stops and many mistakes in grammar. Left to them the English language would die of impurity, like late Latin.

> WANKERS are prissy, fussy, priggish, prim and of what they would probably misrepresent as a higher social class than one's own. They speak in an over-precise way with much pedantic insistence on letters not generally sounded, especially Hs. Left to them the language would die of purity, like medieval Latin.

You come across very few Berks in the modern Latin-reading world, and a lot of Wankers.

Wankers have a proprietorial attachment to archaisms, mostly used by those who want to send out the strong signal— "I know this clever thing and you don't." Wankers will insist on a correct use of Latin in English when it actually ends up sounding ridiculous, e.g.,

> "Do you think that people like me who know Latin tend to be *genii* who should be heard more often in *auditoria?*"
>
> "No, I think most geniuses would think you were a bit of a Wanker and would not want to bloody go near any auditoriums where there was any danger of you turning up."
>
> "Not 'to bloody go.' You've split an infinitive there. 'To go near any bloody *auditoria*' is better."

I rest my case.

Chris Patten, the former MP and Governor of Hong Kong, now the Chancellor of Oxford University, was guilty of classic Wanker's Latin in a review of a history of Balliol College, Oxford, by John Jones in *The Spectator* (January 14, 2006): "The foreword to this edition by the university's recent Vice-Chancellor and Balliol's quondam Master, Colin Lucas," wrote Lord Patten, "draws attention to Balliol's recurrent capacity for being out of tune with the prevailing orthodoxy of the times."

Quondam? *Quondam?*

As a basic rule of thumb you immediately qualify for Wanker's status if you use a Latin word when an English one would do fine. *Quondam* means "former" and there would have been absolutely zero effect lost if Lord Patten had written "Balliol's former Master, Colin Lucas," but then he wouldn't have got that all-important patina (no pun intended in this word, itself a bit of Wanker's Latin, *patina, -ae f.*—a dish or plate, and thus synonymous with the thick green film of oxidation that develops on bronze surfaces) of supposed intelligence and sophistication that comes with using Latin where plain English will do.

Funnily enough, Sir Kingsley's own son, Martin, comes across as a bit of a Wanker in a row the two men once had about the correct use of the word "dilapidated."

The surprisingly literal-minded Martin Amis insisted that "dilapidated" should be used only in its exact sense: *cf. lapis, lapidis m.*—stone, and the verb *dilapido, -are*—to remove stones, from which the past participle *dilapidatus*—having had stones removed. So Martin Amis was saying that you should really only use the word in the sense of, "I wish that truck hadn't careered into that dry-stone wall; it now looks very dilapidated." You could, Martin Amis conceded, use it metaphorically, but only if you had the proper sense in mind.

So—"The Colosseum is looking a bit dilapidated these days," but not, "Kirk Douglas is looking a bit dilapidated these days," because he isn't actually missing any physical part of him, however ropey he might appear.

THE WANKER'S PITFALL

Interestingly, if you use the exact translation of the bit of Latin that an English word is derived from, you are often both a Wanker and *wrong*.

It would be fairly silly, for instance, to insist on using "nebulous" to mean "misty" or "foggy" purely in the meteorological sense of the original Latin adjective (*nebulosus, -a, -um*). And no one could possibly understand you if you used "strata" to mean "blankets," "saddle-cloths," or "pavements," as the Romans did (*stratum, -i, n.*).

That doesn't mean that it isn't intriguing to know the Latin origin of English words, or that it isn't useful show-off material. In fact, the greater the jump in meaning, the more esoteric you'll seem if you can explain the jump without, like a Wanker, becoming attached to the original meaning.

So, while it isn't surprising that *candidus, -a, -um adj.* means "white" and that *candid*, i.e., "pure, unvarnished," is derived from it, the jump to "candidate" is less obvious. The word "candidate" evolved from the fact that Roman candidates for election wore togas covered in white chalk dust to make them stand out in a crowd.

Just as odd is the derivation of *atrium*, meaning, as it did in Latin, "a hall." Atrium is derived from *ater, atra, atrum adj.*— black, since the atrium was where the main wall-blackening fire in a house was.

The Atrium, Greenwich Village, New York—not black

Yes, indeed, being too literal in your English can lead to all sorts of nastiness—not just lots of complicated Latinate words, but also clunky, leaden sentences: "The pirates, bearing malice, will have borne weapons against the soothsayers."

The genius at capturing this stilted idiocy is Molesworth, hero of the Geoffrey Willans and Ronald Searle books. Molesworth gets the constipated feel of badly translated Latin spot on:

The Gauls have attacked the camp with shouts they have frightened the citizens they have killed the enemy with darts and arows and blamed the belgians. They have also continued to march into Italy. Would it not be more interesting if they did something new?

In *The Secret History*, Donna Tartt captures that same awful, literal clumsiness when the narrator, Richard Papen, exhausted by the strain of murdering his classmate, copies a friend's second-rate translation: "Being weary from the march, the soldiers stopped to offer sacrifices at the temple. I came back from that country and said that I had seen the Gorgon, but it did not make me a stone."

That said, for all Tartt's and Molesworth's brilliance in hammering the stunted English that comes from literal translation, there is often beauty in the brevity of the original Latin.

On a sundial in a monastery cloisters on the edge of Venice, an old monk once inscribed: *Horas non numero nisi serenas.* It means literally, "I don't count the hours unless they are serene ones." It also means, "I only tell the time when the sun's out." But it really means, "When I come to die, the only moments that matter will have been the moments when I was at ease." And the joy of the original is increased when you say it out loud. For all its brevity, when you say, "*Horas non numero nisi serenas,*" it sounds like what it is—a rich, distilled, romantic language—the purest, headiest Italian.

THE WANKER'S TRIUMPH

There are times when Latin use in English is not Wankerish, but right. On January 20, 2006, the op-ed page of the *Daily Telegraph* used Latin in a precise, illuminating way that worked better than the equivalent English would have.

The journalist Tom Utley used his Latin in writing about the story in the tabloid *The Sun,* that Fathers 4 Justice, the lobby group for greater access to children for divorced fathers, was planning to kidnap the prime minister's son:

> So the fascinating question arises of who, exactly, wanted that story to appear on the front page of the *Sun? Cui bono?*—as detectives and lawyers used to ask, in the days when Latin was taught more widely than cake decoration in our schools. Who benefits? The first answer, obviously, is the *Sun.* Sensational stories sell newspapers—and, sure enough, the *Sun's* front

page was the only one that BBC2 thought worthy of attention on Wednesday's *Newsnight*.

Cui bono is nicer sounding and more powerful than the English equivalent—"Who benefits?" *Cui bono* also has an added nuance, for those who are familiar with the phrase: it encapsulates the idea of some hidden, often underhand, benefit that you have to do a bit of detective work to discover.

N.B. (*nota bene*—note well) in what a masterly way Mr. Utley here avoids the charge of being called a Wanker, by explaining the use of the expression, i.e., he doesn't do the real Wanker's thing of leaving something in Latin that a lot of readers won't get, in order to show off and say, "I know what this means and you don't, you utter fool."

YOU AT THE BACK, PAY ATTENTION

Anyway, it's time for some more grammar, in particular Second Declension neuter nouns, ending in *-um*, as in *bellum*, *-i*, *n.*—war (as in bellicose). Pronounce "bellum" as "blum," and you get the nice little rhythm, "Blum, blum, blum, bli, blo, blo; bla, bla, bla, bllorum, blis, blis." Just in case this doesn't make any sense, take a look at the full table.

	Singular	**Plural**
NOM.	*bellum*	*bella*
VOC.	*bellum*	*bella*
ACC.	*bellum*	*bella*
GEN.	*belli*	*bellorum*
DAT.	*bello*	*bellis*
ABL.	*bello*	*bellis*

Second Declension nouns: ending in -um

The nice thing about all neuter nouns and adjectives is that they are the same in the nominative, vocative, and accusative, and the same goes for neuter plurals.

THE GREAT MOUNTS — OR THIRD DECLENSION NOUNS

On the dedication page of this book, I've actually got it wrong in calling my brother and sister *Mons Maximus* and *Mons Maxima*. But first, let me explain how these nicknames came about.

For a long time, between 1976 and 1982, my elder brother, William, my younger sister, Mary, and I were all at the same schools, North Bridge House Junior and Senior School, in Hampstead and Regent's Park, respectively, both in north London. And there we started learning Latin.

For a while, in the early days, we enjoyed rude Latin with phrases like *ubi sub ubi* ("where," "under," "wear"—say it

Mons Maximus, Mons, Mons Maxima

quickly); and our favorite made-up verb—*po, pis, pist, pimus, pistis, pants* (say it quickly).

We then graduated to giving each other Latin names. I got called *Mons* (as in *mons, montis, m.*—a mountain). In a couple of pages you'll see how to decline *mons*.

For a few years at prep school, I was just straightforwardly "Mons." But, if my brother, my sister, and I had been at an old-fashioned prep school, we would have been *Mons maior, Mons minor,* and *Mons minima.* My dedication rather ignores the correct hierarchy of age and salutes instead my siblings' shared brilliance of character—*Mons Maximus,* the Greatest Mount (masculine), and *Mons Maxima,* the Greatest Mount (feminine).

You might call this terrible Latin because *mons* is masculine and should never really take a feminine adjective. In any

case, my brother and sister should really be in the dative because the book is dedicated to them as in "To [or for] William
and Mary." So the dedication should read *Monti Maiori et
Monti Minimae*, or even, with the mounts in the plural, *Mon-
tibus Maiori et Minimae* but that doesn't sound as fittingly grand
as *Mons Maximus et Mons Maxima.*

I got the gender of *mons* wrong again and also got the
wrong tense—and was also a bit of a Wanker—when I wrote
an inscription on a bit of Welsh slate to hang over the Flemish
fireplace in the ruined, overgrown cottages cleared out by my
parents next to their unruined cottage in St. Twynnells, Pem-
brokeshire, in Wales.

"The Great Mounts tamed these sylvan ruins,
April 1993"

43

But back to the Third Declension, which in the case of *mons* goes like this:

There are lots of irregular Third Declension nouns so it's not really worth spending too much time going into them.

A good rule of thumb is to count on the nominative being pretty different from the accusative—that's when it jumps into its longer form if it's going to, and then after that it pretty much settles into the familiar rhythm.

	Singular	**Plural**
NOM.	*mons*	*montes*
VOC.	*mons*	*montes*
ACC.	*montem*	*montes*
GEN.	*montis*	*montium*
DAT.	*monti*	*montibus*
ABL.	*monte*	*montibus*

A Third Declension noun

By the way, if you want to start forming English words out of these expanding Third Declension nouns—like *rex*, *regis*, and *mons*, *montis*—that get bigger in the genitive, then you take the root from the longer accusative form: mountain, not mounsain; regicide, not rexicide.

The suffix "-icide" is a useful one, to be added on to anything that's in danger of being murdered. Aborticide is a new word much in vogue among the religious right. It is derived from *caedo*, *-ere*, *cecidi*, *caesum*—I kill.

As ever there are exceptions to the expanding-noun rule. Sometimes a noun gets smaller in the accusative. *Iuppiter*—Jupiter—goes: *Juppiter, Jovem, Jovis, Jovi, Jove.* From which you will see that when Jeeves's master, Bertie Wooster, was heard to swear, "By Jove," he was guilty of a sort of tautology, since Jove (the ablative form of the noun) means "By Jupiter" in the first place.

Actually, while we're on the subject, it's worth having a look at Roman gods . . .

DIANA THE HUNTRESS
AND CAMILLA THE VIRGIN
QUEEN—ROMAN GODS
AND GODDESSES

René Goscinny and Albert Uderzo, the author and artist, respectively, of the *Asterix* books, are here, as so often in the popular French cartoon, spot-on about the little details of the Roman Empire—in this case religion. One of the priorities of Roman colonization was the appropriation of the local gods that were worshiped by the tribes they conquered.

In the little unconquered Brittany village where Asterix and Obelix lived in 50 BC, the Gauls would certainly have worshiped Toutatis, the ancient god of war, fertility, and wealth, before they were conquered. The conquering Romans then gradually introduced some of their own customs—gods, baths, togas—as they did in Roman Britain (*infra*, below).

And little by little, as this top-down influence seeped through the provinces, the lower orders began to imitate their chiefs. There was therefore no need for the Romans to inflict any nasty compulsory conversion: the native gods and habits of the conquered were painlessly absorbed into the new Roman tradition. And the Romans themselves borrowed from previous empires and from the places they colonized. The stories of Hercules were culled from the Greek tales of Heracles and they, in turn, had been borrowed from the stories that pre-Greek tribes had concocted about their own local strong man.

Christianity ended up doing the same with many of its rituals. Christmas is a joint appropriation of the Roman winter festival, Saturnalia, celebrating Saturn, the god of agriculture, and the northern pagan ritual, known as Yule. Yule was a celebration of the birth of the pagan Sun God, Mithras (much appropriated by Roman Britons), and was observed on December 21, the shortest day of the year, when Yule logs were burned and kisses exchanged as a fertility ritual under the mistletoe, the crucial ingredient in Getafix's magic potion in the *Asterix* books.

It wasn't until AD 350 that Pope Julius I declared that Christ's birth would be celebrated on December 25, making it as easy as possible for pagan Romans, the vast majority of Romans, to switch to the new rituals.

With this cross-fertilization between empires and religions, it is no coincidence that the Greek and Roman gods and their powers and stories are so interchangeable.

Here's a list of the main Greek gods and goddesses and their Roman equivalents:

Zeus/Jupiter—King of the gods, free with his lightning bolts

Poseidon/Neptune—God of the sea

Hades/Pluto—God of the underworld

Hestia/Vesta—Goddess of the hearth, symbol of the home, worshiped by the Vestal Virgins

Hera/Juno—Jupiter's wife and, confusingly, sister

Ares/Mars—God of war

Athena/Minerva—The motherless daughter of Zeus who sprang fully formed from his head. The goddess of wisdom; thus London's club for dons and vicars, the Athenaeum, incidentally one of the finest neoclassical buildings in the world, with its frieze copied from the Parthenon.

Apollo/also Apollo—God of the sun. Often depicted with his chariot galloping along, bringing the dawn with him.

Aphrodite/Venus—The goddess of love

Hermes/Mercury—The fleet-footed messenger god, associated with newspapers

Artemis/Diana—Goddess of the moon and hunting. Thus the conclusion to Earl Spencer's funeral tribute to his sister (who, unlike Camilla Parker Bowles, didn't like hunting much) in Westminster Abbey on September 6, 1997:

It is a point to remember that of all the ironies about Diana, perhaps the greatest was this—a girl given the name of the ancient goddess of hunting was, in the end, the most hunted person of the modern age.

Camilla in Roman legend was, by the way, a virgin queen of the Volscians, the daughter of King Metabus. She helped Turnus in his conflict with Aeneas, and was killed in the process.

In the following passage in Book XI (11, cf., Roman numerals, *infra*) of Virgil's *Aeneid*, the goddess Diana describes the death of Camilla, the little royal Amazon with a love of virginity, and explains how she has always loved her:

"Graditur bellum ad crudele Camilla,
O virgo, et nostris nequiquam cingitur armis,
Cara mihi ante alias." Neque enim novus iste Dianae
Venit amor subitaque animum dulcedine movit.

"And so Camilla went off to that cruel war;
She was kitted out with all my weapons but in vain.
She was dearer to me than anyone else."
Diana's love for Camilla wasn't anything new—
It wasn't as if this was the first time that this love had stirred Diana's soul with sweetness.

Aeneid, Book XI

VOCAB.

gradior, gradi, gressus sum—I walk

nequiquam—in vain

cingo, cingere, cinxi, cinctum—I surround, encircle

subitus, -a, -um—sudden

dulcedo, inis f.—sweetness

More gods and goddesses:

Hephaestus/Vulcan—Son of Hera/Juno, god of fire. The only ugly and deformed god. Makes armor and weapons forged in volcanoes.

Gaea/Terra—Mother Earth

Asclepius/Aesculapius—God of medicine

Cronos/Saturn—God of agriculture

Demeter/Ceres—Goddess of grain

Dionysus/Bacchus—God of wine and vegetation

Eros/Cupid—God of love

Hypnos/Somnus—God of sleep

Rhea/Ops—Wife of Cronus/Saturn. The mother goddess.

Uranus/also Uranus—God of the sky and father of the Titans

Nike/Victoria—Goddess of victory. Incidentally, if you want to be a real Wanker, pronounce the popular sports shoe brand as the ancient Greeks did— *Kneekay.*

Anyway, it's time to get back to the nitty-gritty.

FOURTH DECLENSION NOUNS

These are only a little trickier than the Third Declension, the principal pitfall being the fact that they end in *-us*, like Second Declension nouns, i.e., *dominus*, but are declined in an entirely different way.

	Singular	**Plural**
NOM.	*vultus*	*vultus*
VOC.	*vultus*	*vultus*
ACC.	*vultum*	*vultus*
GEN.	*vultus*	*vultuum*
DAT.	*vultui*	*vultibus*
ABL.	*vultu*	*vultibus*

Fourth Declension nouns, vultus, -us m. —face

TUSCAN COLUMNS AND THE HISTORICAL IMPORTANCE OF *MY FAIR LADY*—A QUICK CULTURAL TOUR OF ROME

T o get a rapid hold of Roman architecture, you must learn a rude mnemonic—DICC.

DICC may be the sort of thing taught to you by the annoying teacher who tries to make you like him by taking advantage of the adolescent's obsession with sex and his amusement at rude words.

Still, remember DICC, and you have the boilerplate for all classical architecture from 600 BC to the present day.

Doric, Ionic, Corinthian, and Composite columns—that is, DICC—are the four literal pillars of Roman buildings, although it must be acknowledged that the principles are almost entirely borrowed from the Greeks. DICC gives you the chronology of the orders of architecture—Doric came first, then Ionic, then Corinthian, then Composite. They also grow taller and their capitals (or crests) get more ornate the later they get. And, whenever you get a classical building of more than one floor, the types of column run through the DICC order, the higher you go, i.e., Doric on the first floor, Ionic on the second, etc.

DORIC COLUMNS—SEVENTH CENTURY BC

The Doric column was perfected under Dorus, the ruler of the Peloponnese, who built a temple in the style in Argos, dedicated to Juno.

It is the simplest, chunkiest, and thought to be the most male order, and was said by Vitruvius, the first architectural historian, to be derived from the ratio of the length of a man's foot to his height.

A Doric column bulges in the middle and then tapers to the top, in an architectural trick called entasis. If the line were straight, the eye would tend to think the column was collapsing inwardly; thus the need to compensate in the other direction.

Doric columns are topped with a simple, unadorned round capital. The columns tend to be fluted—that is, they have vertical grooves running up and down them. The best-known examples are the best-known columns in the world, the socking great ones on the Parthenon in Athens.

IONIC COLUMNS—SIXTH CENTURY BC

Thought to be the most feminine of orders, the Ionic order is best spotted through its spreading capital with two scrolls, or volutes, unfurling on either side of it; or, if you prefer, like a girl's curls tucked up on either side of her head.

Ionic columns, like girls, are thin; thinner than the bulky Doric columns. They are about nine times taller than they are wide.

The Ionic order came from the Ionian colonies of Greece on the southwestern shores of Asia Minor (modern Turkey). Its

JUAN MANUEL CAICEDO CARVAJAL

Like pretty young girls: Ionic columns at the
Erechtheum, Athens

finest example is again on the Parthenon, in its side temple—
the Erechtheum.

CORINTHIAN COLUMNS—400 BC

The Corinthian column was first used by the Greeks in 400
BC but was much popularized by the Romans.

The Corinthian capital, heavier and more ornate than

JAMES RYE

From Roman temple to Christian church: the
Corinthian portico of the Pantheon, Rome

JAMES RYE

*Rome's favorite twins: the Corinthian temple of Castor
and Pollux in the Forum*

its predecessors, was the first to use acanthus leaves sprouting
out of the side, with small volutes folding out at the top.

The best-known Corinthian temples are the Pantheon
(built AD 120) and the Temple of Castor and Pollux in the
Forum, both in Rome.

Incidentally, the shallow curve of the roof of the Pantheon
is so sophisticated that modern architectural historians still
don't know how it was built.

Incidentally, again, Castor and Pollux were the twin

gods who Romans thought they saw at their victory over the Etruscans in 496 BC. As a result, the Romans built an early version of this temple in the Forum; it was later rebuilt by the Emperor Tiberius in AD 6.

COMPOSITE COLUMNS—AD 82

The Composite column, the showiest of them all, was the only one actually invented by the Romans, with the upper part of the capital based on the Ionic capital, and the lower part on the Corinthian; thus the word Composite.

The first example of the Composite order is on the Arch of Titus, in the Roman Forum, built in AD 82.

Real swots might also want to take in the Tuscan order, which wasn't invented until the sixteenth century by Italian architectural theorists. This is the simplest order of all, basically a Doric column with a base and no fluting. Because it was so simple to build, the Tuscan column was called Gardener's Doric, easily knocked up to make gateposts and fences.

Architects looking for a simple, consciously ancient effect often plump for the Tuscan order. This was the look Inigo Jones went for in St. Paul, Covent Garden, with its Tuscan pillars and heavy overhanging eaves. The church appears in the opening scenes of the film *My Fair Lady*. Indeed it is under the Tuscan eaves of St. Paul that Professor Higgins meets Eliza Doolittle.

HANS BOUMAN

*A purely Roman building: Composite columns
at the Arch of Titus, Rome*

Roman architecture was so advanced that it wasn't bettered for a thousand years, until the twelfth century, when the French came up with the pointed Gothic arch, which could bear more weight and therefore support taller buildings than previously possible.

It's no coincidence, then, that an alternative word for

STEVE CADMAN

Where Audrey Hepburn met Rex Harrison—
St. Paul, Covent Garden

Norman architecture in Britain is Romanesque—the fact is that William the Conqueror's builders hadn't advanced on the principles of Roman architecture by the time they invaded Britain. And the earliest Norman buildings in Britain—the chapel in the Tower of London, St. Bartholomew's in the City of London, Durham Cathedral—with their round arches and barrel vaulting, could all have been built a thousand years earlier in Rome.

In fact, the very shape of our churches is dictated by Roman architecture and, more precisely, by Roman temples. The idea of a cross-shape was of course a debt to Jesus and the cross. But the concept of a long rectangular nave flanked by aisles, with a semicircular chancel at the end where the altar is, comes from pre-Christian Roman temples.

If you take a walk down Queen Victoria Street in the City of London, you'll find the second century AD Temple of Mithras, originally built underground and now raised on a platform, so workers flooding in from the commuter train station at Cannon Street can get a good look at it.

Mithras was the god of light and sun, worshiped for slaying a primordial bull in a dark cave—thus the tendency to build Mithraea, (as a group of temples to Mithras are called)

ANDREW FINDEN

Pagan church plan—the Temple of Mithras, London

underground—and unleashing the powers of creativity and life in the world.

The nave bit was where Romans, like us, gathered for services, although they tended to sit in the aisles on benches that ran alongside the walls. And the chancel area (from *cancellus, -i, m.*—the railing or screen before the altar) was where sacrifices were burned in Roman pagan rituals.

The influences of Roman architecture on British and Western architecture are too deep and numerous to mention beyond the obvious examples: the triumphal arch (as in Marble Arch) derived from the Arch of Titus in the Roman Forum; the triumphal column (as in Nelson's Column) from Trajan's Column in Rome; modern running tracks from the stadium at Rome; theaters from Marcellus's theater in Rome . . .

There is one particular Roman building, though that is worthy of a special mention—the second century BC Temple of Hercules in Rome, which inspired not only St. Paul's Cathedral in London, St. Peter's in Rome, and the Radcliffe Camera in Oxford, but every dome on a colonnaded drum in the world, including the Capitol in Washington, DC (*infra*).

This temple was once thought to be the Temple of Vesta, originally inhabited by the famous Vestal Virgins—the only female priests in Rome. Their main job was to maintain the sacred fire of Vesta, goddess of the hearth; thus the name Swan Vestas, matches that wouldn't go out easily.

And incidentally, the Vestal Virgins were not that different from the version portrayed in the British farce movie, *Carry on Cleo*. Just as in the film, Vestal Virgins tended to be young—they

MÍCHEÁL Ó FOGHLÚ

The Capitol's inspiration—Temple of Hercules, Rome

started in the temple at any age from three to ten—and were in good physical condition, chosen as they were from grand families, though they presumably got a bit ropey after their thirty years of service, with the first ten spent as novices, the second ten as Vestal Virgins proper, and the last ten as supervisors.

At this point, they were permitted to leave the temple and marry. And Bridget Joneses everywhere will be consoled by their story: even though they were at least thirty-three when they left the temple, they were considered an excellent catch.

The virgins had special privileges: they could look after their own property; they had special seats at the games, while other women had to sit in the back row; and they were generally considered sacred. If a condemned man met a Vestal Virgin on his way to the scaffold, he was pardoned automatically. All this was dependent on them remaining virgins, as *Carry on Cleo* rightly stresses. If they broke their vow of chastity, they were buried alive—to spill a Vestal Virgin's blood was forbidden, even after she'd lost her virginity—in the Campus Sceleratus, the "Wicked Fields," while their lovers were flogged to death. The Vestal Virgins survived until AD 394, when all non-Christian cults were outlawed.

By the way, the Temple of Hercules and the other buildings I have been talking about in Rome are all on or around the Seven Hills of Rome. If you are not familiar with this area, you ought to know that only one of these ancient seven hills of Rome, the Capitoline Hill, properly strikes you as a hill when you go round the city. They were much more obvious as hills before the marshy ravines between them were drained and filled in with buildings.

THE SEVEN HILLS OF ROME

Aventine Hill—The hill where Remus chose to live

Caelian Hill—The Upper East Side of Rome during the Roman Republic, 510–31 BC

Capitoline Hill—The hill of government. The temples of Jupiter Optimus Maximus, Juno Moneta, and Concord were all on the Capitoline.

Esquiline Hill—a quiet hill

Palatine Hill—Romulus's Hill, where he founded the

city after killing his twin brother, Remus. Rome may not have been built in a day, but it was certainly founded by Romulus on a specific one, April 21, 753 BC.

Quirinal Hill—Now home to the Quirinal Palace, a sixteenth-century papal palace, the residence of the kings of Italy from 1870 to 1946 and since then home to the Italian president

Viminal Hill—another quiet hill

If ancient Rome had a powerful effect on British and European architecture, its influence on American architecture was absolutely overwhelming.

You might call Washington, DC, the Imperial City for many good political reasons, but you'd be forcing the point a little. When it comes to architecture, though, the American capital really could slip pretty much unnoticed right into ancient imperial Rome. The capital's Capitol takes its name from the Roman building of the same name, built on top of the Capitoline Hill. Like its Washington, DC, counterpart, the Roman Capitol was also the central hub of government and the symbolic center of the Roman world. The Founding Fathers even went as far as placing their principal government building on a raised piece of ground, like the Romans—thus the political expression "on the hill." And, when it came to looking for a model for the U.S. Capitol, its early architect, William Thornton, didn't stray far from the Roman Capitol—he went just down the Capitoline Hill and borrowed from the second century BC Temple of Hercules (*supra*, see above).

CARPE DIEM

JONATHAN D. COLMAN

The Capitol, Washington, DC

Thornton's model for a central government building spread across America and the world. Cuba's old government building in Havana, El Capitolio (1929), was a direct rip-off of the Capitol. Since the 1959 revolution, Fidel Castro has seen little reason to delegate power to a government of any sort, and so El Capitolio now houses the Cuban Academy of Sciences.

The great imperial architect of Washington, Benjamin Latrobe, who adapted the plans for the Capitol, indulged his love of ancient Rome elsewhere across the country. Latrobe designed several classical buildings in his native England before helping to spread the fashion in America. He was behind the first Catholic cathedral in America, the Baltimore Basilica (1806–21), and, in conjunction with James Hoban, the White House. (The White House, by the way, was built on the banks of a little stream given the grand—and distinctly Roman—name of Tiber Creek.)

65

TOM SKINNER

El Capitolio, Havana

Latrobe was a great one for Americanizing his classical influences, taking Corinthian capitals and inserting corncobs between the leaves. And, for the capitals of the Corinthian columns of the vestibule and rotunda of the Senate wing of the Capitol, he removed acanthus leaves and replaced them with the leaves and flowers of the powerhouse crop of the American economy—the tobacco plant. This taste for classicism in Washington's federal buildings spread through state government, too. From the grandest state capitol in the land, the Massachusetts State House in Boston, designed by Charles Bulfinch in 1795, to the smallest state courthouse, classicism prevailed.

A similar itch for the ancient led to a rash of classical town names, even if they are mostly Greek in origin: Ithaca, New York, broke away from its parent town of Ulysses (founded 1790) in 1821; Athens, Georgia, the university town, was given its name in 1801 in conscious memory of the home of Plato and Aristotle; Troy, New York, was christened in 1789. The trend went on for decades—Sparta, Wisconsin, was named by a keen local lady classicist in 1850.

A trend toward Gothic architecture took off in American religious buildings from the nineteenth century onward—just look at Grace Church, the old and the new St. Patrick's Cathedrals, and St. John the Divine Cathedral in New York, and the Washington National Cathedral in DC.

But government buildings remained resolutely classical. The Federal style, later popularized throughout America, was just a different term for a classical revival. This wasn't just an architectural fad. The Founding Fathers were express in their intention to recall Rome not only in their buildings, but in their politics, too.

The American love of Rome—or, more specifically, Roman Republican virtues—intensified with the birth of the American Republic after the revolution. The Fathers sought a virtuous model of government that could be separated from the monarchy they had just overthrown; the Roman Republic was ideal. Roman Republicanism seemed at one and the same time pure, but not too dangerously democratic. Thomas Jefferson and the two John Adamses were keen on the Greek and Roman idea of rule by the optimates—the best, or, in Jefferson's phrase, a "natural aristocracy" based on the most talented.

But it was in architecture that imperial America reached its apogee. Washington had his own classical home, Mount Vernon, on the outskirts of the city.

JEFFREY PEEDEN

Rome on the Potomac: Mount Vernon

But the iconic figure who intertwined the classical threads of architecture, academia, and politics was Thomas Jefferson (1743–1826). In politics, he yearned to replicate the ideals of the Roman Republic in the new American Republic. As an architect, he was an obsessive Romanist. It was Jefferson who, when he was Secretary of State, insisted that Washington's federal buildings should be classical. And it was Jefferson who in 1791 advised Pierre Charles L'Enfant—the architect who designed the grid and diamond plan for Washington, DC, and remodeled New York's Federal Hall with its Doric portico—to follow classical designs for the Capitol: "I should prefer the

SARA BLOGG

A classical education—Jefferson's Rotunda at the
University of Virginia

adoption of some one of the models of antiquity, which have had the approbation of thousands of years."

Jefferson was responsible, too, for the University of Virginia in Charlottesville, distinguished by its central rotunda, a half-size version of the Pantheon in Rome.

Jefferson's other great building was the Virginia State Capitol in Richmond, boasting a handsome great portico. This capitol was inspired by the Augustan temple in Nîmes in the south of France, the so-called Maison Carrée, or Square House.

Jefferson saw the Maison Carrée on a grand tour of Europe

69

PETER WENDEL

Jefferson the copycat—the Maison Carrée, Nîmes

in 1787. He was "nourished with the remains of Roman grandeur," he said.

So in love was Jefferson that he engaged the leading French architect and archaeologist, Jacques-Louis Clérisseau, to make sketches and models of the Maison Carrée to help his designs for the Virginia Capitol.

Jefferson's masterpiece, though, was Monticello, near Charlottesville, which has a pretty good claim to the title of most influential building in America. Built on top of an 850-foot mountain (Monticello means "little mountain" in Italian), the house is a little bit of Rome in the Virginian mountains, stuffed by Jefferson with cases and cases of antiquities. Monticello is built in the Palladian style, following the

LINDA PRESSON

Jefferson's little mountain—Monticello

rules of Andrea Palladio, the Italian architect (1508–80), whose own rules derived from ancient Roman buildings.

Although Palladianism had originally come from Italy, it had gone through an English incarnation—with its great buildings sponsored by the Whig aristocracy. Jefferson much admired the Whig Enlightenment ideals of political liberty and republican civic virtue and in turn admired Whig architecture.

Even when it came to dress, Romans provided the inspiration. The Rome obsession is beautifully caught in this Charles Willson Peale picture of William Pitt, who, although an English politician, was an American hero. The picture was

71

paid for by a group of Virginia planters, delighted with Pitt's fight to repeal the Stamp Act, which taxed any American deal involving printed paper.

Pitt is painted as a consul in the Roman Republic—a costume that took off among Americans in the following years.

William Pitt's first toga party

As Peale, who became one of the leading portraitists in late-eighteenth-century America, said, "A good painter of either portrait or History, must be well acquainted with the Greesian and Roman statues."

In another painting, by John Singleton Copley, of the revolutionary Massachusetts governor and Founding Father Samuel Adams, the traditional pose of the Roman Republican senator is evoked. Painted in 1770–2, it shows Adams shortly after the Boston Massacre of March 5, 1770, when five civilians were killed by British troops. Adams gestures toward the

MUSEUM OF FINE ARTS, BOSTON

The Revolution is brewing—Sam Adams,

Roman senator

73

seal of Massachusetts and the charter of William and Mary, which granted the state privileges that had been abused in the massacre. In his other hand, he holds a petition signed by Bostonians protesting the killings.

The fashion for all things Roman continued after the American Revolution. Washington's celebrity and triumphs meant that the passion for Rome deviated from a passion for Republican Rome to a cult of Imperial Rome. Washing-

METROPOLITAN MUSEUM OF ART

Emperor Washington

74

ton, who did his best to limit the powers of the new presidency, did not encourage the cult but he could do little to stop it.

The bust of Washington by Giuseppe Ceracchi shows Washington dressed like a Roman emperor—a Hadrian or a Marcus Aurelius—his toga pinned at his right shoulder by the traditional rosette brooch. He could hardly look more Roman, or more imperial. Gone is the traditional wig, replaced by the fashionably short hair of Roman emperors. His wide, strong torso and the incised eyes are all borrowed from ancient Roman sculptures. All that's familiar from the famous Gilbert Stuart pictures are the lips, pursed with the pain of Washington's badly fitting false teeth.

JOHN BELUSHI'S ROMAN INFLUENCES

The intense classical nature of American academia predated Jefferson. The central position of Latin and Greek in a young man's education—and it was almost entirely young men—was established with the first schools and universities in the seventeenth century. Boston Latin School, founded in 1635, was America's original great school—still around today, still a public school, and still teaching classics. As its name implies, the Latin School was devoted to teaching the classics, like the great English schools that inspired it. The birth of the private prep school—and, by descent, the preppy—was thanks also to a love of classics. Boston's Roxbury Latin School (1645) and New York's Collegiate School (1645)—both still prep schools today—were originally classics academies.

A Roman aura pervades at Ivy League universities, too—just look at Harvard Yard, with its freshman dorms, libraries, and classrooms, all built in an austere classical style. At their heart is Massachusetts Hall (1720), the oldest academic building in America—again the classical style prevails.

Classics dominated the early curriculums (or curricula, if you want to be a Wanker) of the earliest American universities, too. Some say that the term Ivy League comes not from the creepers clinging to the ancient walls of these seats of learning, but from the Roman numerals, as in the IV League— the Big Three, Harvard, Princeton, and Yale—and a fourth that varies according to the university of the person who claims that theirs is the fourth member. Seven of the eight in the League were founded in the colonial period (Cornell is the odd one out). So it's no surprise that they reflect the academic priorities of English universities at the time, with a heavy emphasis on the study of classics.

Brown (founded 1764), Columbia (1754), Cornell (1865), Dartmouth College (1769), Harvard (1636), Princeton (1746), the University of Pennsylvania (1740), and Yale (1701)—all of them held the study of the classical languages among their founding principles.

All of them, except for Cornell, have Latin mottoes, too. Harvard's is just *Veritas*—"Truth." Dartmouth's—*Vox clamantis in deserto*, "The voice of one crying in the wilderness"—is a little scarier for the first-week freshman. Penn's motto—*Leges sine moribus vanae*, "Laws without morals are useless"—is derived from *Horace*, Book 3, Ode 24: *Quid leges sine moribus vanae proficiunt?*—"What good are laws without morals?" Its original motto—*Sine moribus vanae*—was changed after a wry classicist pointed out that it could be taken to mean "Loose women without morals."

FRAT BOYS AND SOR GIRLS

Fraternities and sororities, with their phi beta kappas or whatever their distinguishing letters might be, are of course more Greek than Roman. Their roots, though, are, more broadly, classical.

The organizations derive their names from the Latin for brother (*frater, fratris m.*) and sister (*soror, sororis f.*). The terms can be used of all sorts of clubs—the Elks are a fraternity. But they are best known in their university incarnation.

First of the university fraternities was the Phi Beta Kappa Society, founded on December 5, 1776, at the College of William and Mary in Williamsburg, Virginia. Phi Beta Kappa was set up by students who hadn't been able to get into the college's prestigious Flat Hat Club (among its members, one Thomas Jefferson). Many of the fraternity rituals were borrowed from the Flat Hat Club, which had been set up in 1750. Flat Hat members used to go to the rough Raleigh Tavern in downtown Williamsburg, drink heavily, and mix with local sailors and soldiers. The university authorities disapproved and sent out scouts to track down the members. To avoid the scouts, members came up with their own secret handshakes, oaths, and passwords—practices copied by members of Phi Beta Kappa and succeeding fraternities in later years.

The rejects' club, Phi Beta Kappa, was an altogether more serious organization—perhaps that's why its members didn't get into the frivolous Flat Hat—and began by calling itself a literary fraternity. Greek studies so filled their minds that they took the name Phi, Beta, and Kappa, from the initials of a Greek motto: *philosophia biou kubernetes*—"Love of wisdom, the guide of life."

Despite the Greek name, the Phi Beta Kappa Society gathered to mull over highbrow topics that weren't taught at the classics-obsessed university. Perhaps because of this serious side, the fashion for fraternities only built slowly and it took nearly half a century before they mutated into the social organizations they are today.

The Chi Phi frat, founded in Princeton in 1824, was the first social club. Then the craze mushroomed, with the Kappa Alpha Society following the next year at Union College, Schenectady, New York. Literary interests fell by the wayside; the fostering of friendship was the principal aim of Kappa Alpha and its Union College offspring, Sigma Phi and Delta Phi. This was the jumping-off point for nationwide fraternities, with Sigma Phi spawning a satellite chapter at Hamilton College in Clinton, New York, in 1831.

From then on, America went Greek-mad, with chapters opening in universities across America: Zeta Psi (1847) at New York University launched a chapter on the other side of the country at the University of California, Berkeley (1870), and by 1889 had chapters at all the Ivy League schools.

After a dip in popularity during the Civil War, fraternities boomed again, and the growth has continued ever since,
both in terms of the number of chapters and their members. In
2005, Dartmouth College had 1,785 students who were members of a fraternity, sorority, or a coed Greek house—60 percent of the total student body. The University of Illinois, the
Greekest campus on earth, has forty-six fraternities and
twenty-three sororities.

Sororities began during the mid-nineteenth-century fraternity boom. The Adelphean Society at the Wesleyan College, Macon, Georgia, was the first (1851), quickly followed
the next year by the college's Philomathean Society (*philomathean* being the Greek for "love of learning"). It took a
while for these to emulate the fraternities and take on Greek
initials—the Adelphean Society and the Philomathean Society became Alpha Delta Pi and Phi Mu in 1904.

These early clubs weren't yet called sororities—they got
given the oxymoronic (for "oxymoron," see "Golden Latin—
How to Write Like Cicero," *infra*) name, "women's fraternities."
Not until 1874 was the first Greek-letter sorority, Gamma Phi
Beta, founded at Syracuse University in Syracuse, New York.

TOGA, TOGA, TOGA

Confusingly, given the Greek origins of the fraternity, the
toga is a Roman garment; in fact it was looked upon as a distinctive mark of Roman citizenship from the third century
BC, and non-Romans were forbidden to wear them.

Togas were strictly a men-only thing; women wore the *stola*—a long-sleeved, pleated dress. Memo to all female undergrads before your next toga party—the Romans thought women who wore togas were prostitutes.

A proper toga takes an enormous twenty-foot length of cloth, made of wool, wrapped around the body, with a tunic beneath. The idea was that you could take it off when you were indoors or doing hard, manual work, without being completely naked. In time, the toga grew baggier and baggier as fashion dictated that pragmatics should give way to style. It became impractical to wear for war or physical exercise (or dancing at toga parties—see *The Official Preppy Handbook, infra*). The *sagum*—or woollen cloak—took the toga's place on the battlefield. And the *laena*—or buttoned cloak—became more popular on the viae of Rome. Only in late-twentieth-century America did the fashion for togas return, as a useful, easy-access garment for college-based debauchery.

The origins of the toga party are lost in the alcoholic mists of time. It appears that the parties began in the early years of the twentieth century as a natural offshoot from fraternities' Greek roots. In the early '30s, Eleanor Roosevelt held a toga party at the White House to tease the journalists and politicians who had conceived of her husband as a second Caesar.

Toga parties really only took off after *Animal House* (1978). The party in the movie was inspired by the memories of one of the film's writers, Harold Ramis, who had been a member of the Zeta Beta Tau fraternity at Washington University, St. Louis. The film's toga party scene is crucial to the plot.

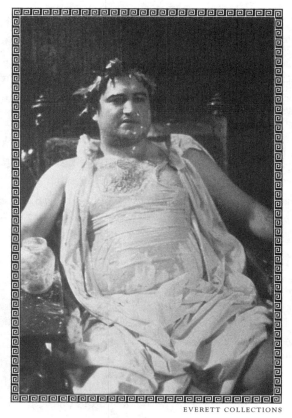

EVERETT COLLECTIONS

John Belushi—keen classicist

The Deltas, the worst frat at Faber College in 1962—as op-posed to the best, the Omegas—are on double secret probation because the college dean hates them so much. Thinking that things can't get much worse, they decide to at least have the ul-timate good time (cf. "to boldly go where no man has gone before," why split infinitives are okay, *infra*) before they are disbanded.

With Bluto Blutarsky, played by John Belushi, at the helm, the party hits new depths of bad behavior. The innocent freshman Larry Kroger (played by Tom Hulce of *Amadeus* fame), pledge name "Pinto," debates with the devil and angel on his shoulders whether to take advantage of the mayor's comatose underage daughter. The dean's drunken wife crashes the party and sleeps with the smooth reprobate, Otter. The dean revokes the fraternity's charter and removes everything from Delta house, "even the stuff we didn't steal!"

Shortly after the movie came out, *Newsweek* did a feature on the toga party, and universities went crazy for the idea: emulating John Belushi and his fellow Deltas, 10,000 University of Wisconsin students dressed themselves in bed sheets and laurel wreaths for a huge party in late 1978. Belushi and several of the other actors from the movie took to turning up unannounced at campus parties.

By the time of the publication of *The Official Preppy Handbook* (1980), only two years later, toga parties had become an acknowledged part of university life. The handbook gives this stern advice, "Toga party—Girls wear designer sheets, men wear the kind from the linen service. If accompanied by a Roman-style dinner, these sheets may go home stained with red wine, though serious drinkers might switch to a grain alcohol punch around 10 o'clock. Since dancing in a toga is impossible, getting drunk is the primary activity."

FIFTH DECLENSION NOUNS

These are thin on the ground, but those that do crop up tend to crop up a lot. The most familiar are *dies, diei f.*—day, and *res, rei f.*—thing. *Res* is a tricky word. The classic translation is "thing" but actually that's usually the last thing it means.

It can mean "matter," particularly when used in the ablative, as in *re*, meaning "in the matter of." This is a use seemingly now confined to office memos: "Re paper clips in the eleventh floor conference room: HR is using too many of them."

Perhaps a better all-purpose word for *res* is "affair," as in *respublica*, meaning "public affairs," coming to mean the state. The proper name for the Roman state was *Senatus Populusque Romanus*—"the Senate and the Roman People" (*que*, when tagged onto the end of a noun, means "and," whereas *et*, the more general word for "and," is used to connect clauses and phrases—confusingly).

Senatus Populusque Romanus is neatly shortened to SPQR, the words stitched into every legionnaire's tassel-edged flag when he sailed across the Channel to Pevensey in Sussex to invade England. The letters are still all over Rome, on monuments, cab doors, and drain covers.

A rebus, by the way, is a representation of a word or a phrase by symbols: i.e., two gates and a head are the municipal shorthand rebus for Gateshead—in northeast England—on town hall buildings. It is derived from the expression *Non verbis sed rebus*—"Not by words, but by things."

MATT PESOTSKI

And here is how to decline *res*:

	Singular	Plural
NOM.	*res*	*res*
VOC.	*res*	*res*
ACC.	*rem*	*res*
GEN.	*rei*	*rerum*
DAT.	*rei*	*rebus*
ABL.	*re*	*rebus*

A Fifth Declension noun

THE GERUND AND THE GERUNDIVE

Gerundives are held up as the oddest thing about Latin because, some claim, there is no English equivalent.

Kingsley Amis says of the gerundive, "Fowler says there is no gerundive in English, only a participle. He writes 2,000 words on the gerund alone. In my experience you will not get very far with the gerund or the gerundive unless you know Latin, nor a great deal further if you do."

I'm not sure if either Fowler or Sir Kingsley is right.

The gerund is a verbal noun, i.e., a way of turning a verb into a noun: so the gerund of "I love" is "loving" and the gerund of "I do" is "doing." In "Making love is quite an art," "making love" is a gerund.

Making gerunds (another gerund, incidentally) is perfectly easy. You simply add *-ndum* to the end of a verb, to get:

---

amandum—loving
monendum—warning
regendum—ruling
audiendum—hearing

The gerund

All of these gerunds decline like the noun *bellum*, *-i*, *n.*—war, e.g.,

Quid mihi tam multas laudando, Basse,
puellas mutatum domina cogis abire mea?

Why are you forcing me to chuck my mistress and change her, Bassus, by praising [*laudando*—gerund] so many other girls?
Propertius, *Elegies IV*

VOCAB.
laudo, -are—I praise
puella, -ae f.—girl
muto, -are—I change
domina, -ae f.—mistress
cogo, -ere, coegi, coactum—I force
abeo, -ire, -ii, -itum—I go away

The gerundive is a little more confusing but all the more wonderful when you know it.

It's a verbal adjective, meaning "*needing* to be kissed/electrocuted/glued," and, as a verbal adjective, declines like a normal adjective, i.e., *magnus, -a, -um adj.*—great.

---

amandus, -a, -um—needing to be loved
monendus, -a, -um—needing to be warned
regendus, -a, -um—needing to be ruled
audiendus, -a, -um—needing to be heard

The gerundive

A gerundive is used in a precisely Latin way in English by John Mortimer's Rumpole of the Bailey, who knows some classics, and calls his wife, "She who must be obeyed."

The name Amanda is also a gerundive, meaning "A girl who must be loved." "Agenda" is strictly a gerundive, from *ago, agere, egi, actum*—"I do, carry out." So "agenda" literally means "things that need to be done." If you wanted to be a Wanker, and there was only one item to be dealt with at your next office meeting, you could quite correctly say, "What an interesting agendum we have before us today."

When you add it to the verb "to be," the gerundive can also be used to mean "I must . . . massage/giggle/whatever":

Nunc est bibendum
"Now, we must drink" (literally, "it is to be drunk")
Horace, *Odes 18,*
The Blessings and Dangers of Wine

BERTIE WOOSTER'S CLASSICAL EDUCATION—LATIN IN ENGLISH LITERATURE

To trace the influence of Latin on English literature would take a longer and more serious book than this.

Enough, then, to point to the three great Latin influences on English literature: first, the great number of story lines taken from Roman myth and Roman history (which had an equally vast effect on Renaissance painters and sculptors); second, the classical education that most educated men had in Europe from AD 1100 to 1900; and finally, Christianity.

Take Shakespeare. Ben Jonson said he had "small Latin and less Greek," but even Shakespeare, a man of relatively humble origins who didn't go to university, did know a little of both.

Shakespeare's education at the King's New School in Stratford-upon-Avon would have consisted almost entirely of translating Latin into English and vice versa. His principal textbook would have been William Lily's *Short Introduction of Grammar*, authorized by Henry VIII as the only grammar book to be used in schools.

It's no surprise, then, that Shakespeare's plays are full of classical stories, history, and references. *Julius Caesar, Coriolanus, Antony and Cleopatra,* and *Titus Andronicus* are the most obvious examples. *The Comedy of Errors* was even based on a Roman comedy, Plautus's *The Twin Brothers*.

I could go on. Dante, Milton, Dryden, Pope, Samuel Johnson—Latin translations and Roman myths and histories were the wellspring of much of their work. Renaissance and Reformation comedy got so tangled up with its Latin roots that writers started recasting—and Christianizing—classical texts to suit the moral and religious outlook of the day.

Schonaeus's *Terentius Christianus* took the place of the original Terence in classrooms. Alexander Nowell drafted new prologues for Terence's *Eunuchus* for performance at Westminster School in 1545, turning bawdy scenes of prostitution into moral examples of how not to behave. As he wrote,

Hinc meretricum sordes, ingluviem rapacitatem nullo periculo, multa cum utilitate tamenque voluptae minori cognoscas, et ubi noris perpetuo oderis.

You'll learn about filthy tarts from this play, their gluttony and greed, but with no danger; instead it'll be incredibly useful and enjoyable because once you've heard all about it, you'll hate it for ever.

For half a millennium, up until the nineteenth century, Latin was the mark of the educated man, and an Oxford education meant a classical education.

In Oxford in the seventeenth century, a lazy undergraduate called Tom Brown (1663–1704) was on the verge of being expelled, when John Fell (1625–1686, Dean of Christ Church and Bishop of Oxford) offered to spare him if he could translate a Martial epigram on the spot.

Here is Martial's couplet, followed by Brown's *ex tempore* ("from the time," off the cuff) translation:

Non amo te, Sabidi, nec possum dicere quare;
Hoc tantum possum dicere, non amo te.

I do not love thee, Doctor Fell,
The reason why I cannot tell;
But this alone I know full well,
I do not love thee, Doctor Fell.

Good old Dr. Fell let Tom stay on, only for him to drop out later and fail to take his degree.

ECCE, JEEVES

This mingling of Latin into the education of English writers and their works went on at full tilt until a century ago.

In his recent biography *Wodehouse: A Life* (2004), Robert McCrum wrote about the extreme influence of classics on the writer, who won a senior classical scholarship at Dulwich College in 1897.

In 1969, McCrum reports, an Oxford classicist wrote to Wodehouse after he'd noticed a similarity between Terence's *The Self-Tormentor* and Wodehouse's *The Luck of the Bodkins*. The undergraduate asked him if Plautus or Terence had been an influence.

Wodehouse wrote back, "There certainly is a great resemblance between the two passages, and it can only be explained by a similarity of thought between us, for though in my time at Dulwich we read a great many authors, for some reason neither Plautus nor Terence came my way. Why would this be? Because P and T were supposed to be rather low stuff? . . . But we read Aristophanes who was just as slangy as either of them."

Certainly Bertie Wooster is forever drawing from the classical education he had at Harrow and Magdalen College, Oxford, at the turn of the nineteenth century. As Bertie says in *Right Ho, Jeeves* (1934), "This done, I retired to an armchair and put my feet up, sipping the mixture with carefree enjoyment, rather like Caesar having one in his tent the day he overcame the Nervii."

And, in *The Girl on the Boat* (1922), Wodehouse gives a

Latin lesson that wouldn't disgrace the most fastidious of classics masters:

> Nothing is more curious than the myriad ways in which the reaction from an unfortunate love affair manifests itself in various men.
>
> No two males behave in the same way under the spur of the female fickleness. *Archilochum*, for instance, according to the Roman writer, *proprio rabies armavit iambo*. It is no good pretending out of politeness that you know what that means, so I will translate. "*Rabies*—his grouch—*armavit*—armed—*Archilochum*—Armilochus—*iambo*—with the iambic—*proprio*—his own invention."
>
> In other words, when the poet Archilochus was handed his hat by the lady of his affections, he consoled himself by going off and writing satirical verse about her in a new metre which he had thought up immediately after leaving the house. That was the way the thing affected him.

THE LATIN-RITE CHURCH

The Old Testament may have been written in Hebrew, the New in Greek, but it was in Latin that the medieval priest principally read and in Latin that he spoke in church.

It is in the translation from the Latin, too, that worshipers were used to hearing the liturgy. That was before the *Book of Common Prayer* was edged out by the 1980 *Alternative Service Book* and the 2000 *Common Worship* series.

Confusingly, the Roman Catholic Church used a Greek liturgy for several hundred years before adopting Latin, but it was the Latin version that stuck until Vatican II in 1962–5.

Vatican II pushed the Catholic liturgy away from direct use of Latin and from translations that remained faithful to the original Latin. How gratifying then that John Paul II reversed the trend when he signed off the 2001 directive, known as *Liturgiam Authenticam*, demanding translations that were closer to Latin. (How gratifying, too, that the new Pope, Benedict XVI, has also backed the use of more Latin in services.)

In America, Australia, Scotland, England, and Wales, bishops have now voted to accept the Vatican-backed translations.

So, in America for example, the prayer before communion, which had gone "Lord, I am not worthy to receive you," will go "Lord, I am not worthy that you should enter under my roof." That's much closer to the original Latin—*"Domine, non sum dignus, ut intres sub tectum meum."*

Likewise, in the Nicene Creed, "born of the Virgin Mary" will revert to "incarnate of the Virgin Mary" (*"incarnatus . . . ex Maria Virgine"*).

And, in the exchange between priest and congregation:

PRIEST: "The Lord be with you."
CONGREGATION: "And also with you."

will become:

> PRIEST: "The Lord be with you."
> CONGREGATION: "And with your spirit."

> PRIEST: *"Dominus Vobiscum."*
> CONGREGATION: *"Et cum spiritu tuo."*

TO ALL THE SIRS I'VE LOVED BEFORE—LATIN TEACHERS I HAVE KNOWN

🔲🔲🔲🔲🔲

Almost twenty years after I left the classroom, I realize that Latin teachers are not the dry, old sticks I thought they were when I was filled with the cynical idiocy of youth. Latin teachers may grow old and dusty, and they may take to cardigans and brown flared suits by the time they have taught classics for twenty years in a minor prep school on the fringes of Tring.

But they remain romantics.

I never saw my last prep school Latin teacher, Dr. Rutherford, so transported to a different era, and to a deeper chamber of his soul, than when he read out the Catullus poem that he must have recited to the upper sixth for ten autumns in a row, after games, just before dusk on a Thursday afternoon.

We had been playing soccer on the frozen mud pitches in the shadow of the mosque where Baker Street meets Regent's Park, not far from Sherlock Holmes's apartment. Back at the school—a white stucco Nash terraced house by the park—my little twelve-year-old fingers were so cold that it was hard to do up the buttons on my white shirt and knot my turquoise tie in the few minutes we had before Dr. Rutherford came through the door.

A bachelor in his mid-thirties who had never gotten the don's job at Cambridge he had coveted as an undergraduate, he was a volatile man whose moods shifted from anger at having to teach half-dressed twelve-year-olds to joy at being able to link his job to his love of Latin.

"Christ, why aren't you ready yet, Upper 6 EJ?" Dr. Rutherford shouted as he came through the door.

"Sorry, sir," said Aron Lowder, the class hard man who combined a shrewd understanding of man's behavior with a lack of interest in his intellectual achievements.

"Any chance of some Catullus while we finish dressing?"

"Don't be insolent, Lowder," said Dr. Rutherford, his face softening. "We're due to do Cincinnatus and his plow today, and that's what we'll do, but, since Mount is still bare-chested, I suppose there's time . . ."

"Oh, wicked, sir!" said Aron, leaning back in his chair, and flicking off the switch of his mind for the next five minutes.

"*Vivamus, mea Lesbia, atque amemus*," began Dr. Rutherford, his hands tucked behind his back, his eyes staring out of the

Regency window, fixed on the gleaming cream John Nash classical villas in the Park,

Rumoresque senum severiorum
omnes unius aestimemus assis.
soles occidere et redire possunt:
nobis cum semel occidit brevis lux,
nox est perpetua una dormienda.
da mi basia mille, deinde centum,
dein mille altera, dein secunda centum,
deinde usque altera mille, deinde centum.
dein, cum milia multa fecerimus,
conturbabimus illa, ne sciamus,
aut ne quis malus invidere possit,
cum tantum sciat esse basiorum.

Here is Ben Jonson's translation:

"Let's live and love: To Lesbia"

Let us live, my Lesbia
and let us judge all the rumours of the old men
to be worth just one penny!
The suns are able to fall and rise:
When that brief light has fallen for us
we must sleep a never-ending night.
Give me a thousand kisses, then another hundred,
then another thousand, then a second hundred,

then yet another thousand more, then another hundred.
Then, when we have made many thousands,
we will mix them all up so that we don't know
and so that no one can be jealous of us when he finds
out how many kisses we have shared.

When Dr. Rutherford got to the crux of the poem—
"Give me a thousand kisses, then another hundred . . ." "*Da mi
basia mille, deinde centum, dein mille altera*" (Say it out loud, and
you'll see what I mean)—he might have been a whip-thin Italian ragamuffin on the backstreets of Naples serenading a
Norwegian Valkyrie in a bikini on her year off; not a thirty-
five-year-old bachelor in a checked shirt and Harris tweed
jacket.

Even more extraordinary, *mirabile dictu* ("wonderful to
say," but say it out loud, and hear how much lovelier it is in
Latin), he could do all this while his angry gaze was transferred
to Aron Lowder at the back of the class, now engrossed in ap-
plying sideburns, mullet, and baseball cap to the profile of Virgil on the front of his *Aeneid I* textbook.

I'm sure that Rutherford had once dreamed of saying the
same lines, when he was not much older than Aron Lowder, to
the unattainably lovely peach in the sixth form, or perhaps
even to a girl at the girls' school down the road.

I have had several types of classics teacher. However broken down they've been, however thick the layers of dandruff
flakes on their shoulders, however deeply buried in them the
lissome eighteen-year-old who once lisped Catullus snippets to

a lover, horizontal in the back of a punt on Cambridge's River Cam, they all held on to a passion for Latin . . .

Richard Conner—a brilliant Cambridge scholar in his late forties, who'd had a car crash shortly before coming to teach at my prep school and still had a forehead pockmarked with cuts. Mr. Conner had a Darwinian view of individual capabilities.

"Lowder," he barked one morning, "you'll never get the hang of Horace. Much better use of your time to come up here and pick the scabs off my forehead."

"Everyone else, '*Dulce et decorum est.*' What does it mean, Fussell?"

"Erm, not entirely sure, sir."

This brilliant man then turned his bloody forehead away from Lowder and in the direction of the London Zoo, on the other side of Regent's Park.

Eyes glazed and focused on the middle distance, he re-cited Horace softly, translating as he went, line by line, to ten transfixed twelve-year-old boys.

Lowder crept back to his chair. Even Lowder, who had by now spent a year turning the cover of his *Aeneid* into a Woodstock scene—with Virgil on stage accompanied by Janis Joplin—stopped coloring in Virgil's dangly pearl earring.

> *Dulce et decorum est pro patria mori:*
> *mors et fugacem persequitur virum*
> *nec parcit inbellis iuventae*
> *poplitibus timidove tergo.*

How sweet and lovely it is to die for your country,
And death pursues even the man who flees
Nor spares the hamstrings or cowardly backs
Of battle-shy youths.

"Of course, bloody Wilfred Owen ripped the line off for his poem, *Dulce et Decorum Est*, in 1917. Got shot a fortnight before the Armistice. Serves him bloody right. That's what happens to boys who plagiarize. *Lowder!* That means you. And Virgil would never have worn a batik scarf."

Still you sensed that Mr. Conner did care at least a little for Owen, as he continued:

Bent double, like old beggars under sacks,
Knock-kneed, coughing like hags, we cursed
    through sludge,
Till on the haunting flares we turned our backs
And towards our distant rest began to trudge.
Men marched asleep. Many had lost their boots
But limped on, blood-shod. All went lame; all blind;
Drunk with fatigue; deaf even to the hoots
Of tired, outstripped Five-Nines that dropped behind.

Mr. Conner was now shouting at us,

Gas! Gas! Quick, boys!—An ecstasy of fumbling,
Fitting the clumsy helmets just in time;
But someone still was yelling out and stumbling,

And flound'ring like a man in fire or lime . . .
Dim, through the misty panes and thick green light,
As under a green sea, I saw him drowning.
In all my dreams, before my helpless sight,
He plunges at me, guttering, choking, drowning.
If in some smothering dreams you too could pace
Behind the wagon that we flung him in,
And watch the white eyes writhing in his face,
His hanging face, like a devil's sick of sin;
If you could hear, at every jolt, the blood
Come gargling from the froth-corrupted lungs,
Obscene as cancer, bitter as the cud
Of vile, incurable sores on innocent tongues,
My friend, you would not tell with such high zest
To children ardent for some desperate glory,
The old Lie; *Dulce et decorum est*
Pro patria mori.

"Owen didn't think much of Horace, did he? But what do you think, boys? Is it a lie? Is it a lie of Mrs. Thatcher to send the Task Force to the Falklands? Well is it, Lowder? I'll give you a clue. *No, it bloody well isn't!*"

Dr. Cedric Meadows—an Old Etonian scholar, whose diffident, distracted air turned to anger at the shortcomings of thirteen-year-old boys.

"Oh, Lowder, you're incorrigible. What's that from? Anyone? Keiko?"

"Erm, *corrigo*—I correct, sir," said Hiroshi Keiko, a silent Japanese boy who only opened his mouth to give perfect answers to teachers, in Maths, Latin, Physics, Chemistry, French, and English comprehension, but not, thank God, in English composition.

"Therefore incorrigible means?" asked Dr. Meadows.

"Incorrectible, sir?"

"Good. But more colloquial, please . . . Mount?"

"Unchangeable?"

"Not quite right . . ."

"Intolerable?"

"Better . . ."

"Unbearable."

"Spot on, Keiko. Gold star for being so clever."

Under his breath, Lowder whispered to Keiko, across the classroom, "Wanker, wankeris. Third Declension, masculine. Meaning? *You.*"

Roger Harvey—an avuncular teacher, who taught so many subjects—Latin, Greek, Russian, General Studies—that it was unlikely that he was ever going to be an expert in any of them.

"Sir, sir. When do you use the infinitive to mean 'to do' something and when do you use the subjunctive?"

"Ah, excellent question, Warshaw. Very, very easy to slip up on this one. Sometimes you need to use the infinitive to mean 'to do' something; sometimes you use the subjunctive."

"Yes, sir, but I still don't quite get it."

It is the Mr. Harveys of this world—who love teaching but haven't actually got much to teach—who are the easiest to lure away from work. The Willans and Searle character, Nigel Molesworth, is again the master of the type:

> "What is the use of latin sir?"
> "er well er quite simple molesworth. latin is er classics you kno and classics are—well they are er—they are the studies of the ancient peoples. er latin gives you not only the history of Rome but er (happy inspiration) its culture, it er tells you about interesting men like J.Caesar, hannibal, livy, Romulus remus and er lars porsena of clusium."

Of all these school masters, Rutherford was perhaps the closest we got to that model classics teacher—the one who never married, because he is married to his subject; the one who, if he did marry, might take advantage of the new British civil partnership dispensation adopted by Sir Elton John and David Furnish—although we neither knew nor cared about his sexual inclinations then.

Our parents might have made a quick mental calculation, balancing Dr. Rutherford's brilliance as a teacher against his penchant for playing duets with boys on the grand piano squeezed into his bachelor flat, before deciding, "Well, if Harry gets into Winchester, he'll come across plenty more people like that, anyway."

My parents certainly couldn't have cared less when I

told them one evening what Dr. Rutherford had told me that afternoon after our Latin prose class.

"Do you know, Mount, how I judge whether I like people?"

"No, sir."

"Well, I think about playing a duet with them and, do you know, sometimes, when you're playing a duet with somebody, you have to reach round their back to hit the high notes?"

"No, sir."

"Well, I'd feel very uncomfortable reaching round the back of, say, Mr. Harvey."

"Yes, sir."

"But I'd feel perfectly at ease playing a duet with you, Mount."

" 'Fraid I don't play the piano, sir."

"That's not really the point . . ."

Dr. Rutherford's desires—for Latin, and perhaps for the boys who studied it—may have been strong, but he generally did his best to conceal them behind a cold, hard exterior. Occasionally, he would adopt a consciously laddish pose—"Phwoarrh, I saw *The Dukes of Hazzard* over the weekend, boys. That Daisy Duke . . ."

It was Dr. Rutherford who gave me my first glass of sherry—some warm *fino*, after Greek poetry—at the age of twelve. It was Dr. Rutherford who first took me, and a group of thirteen-year-olds, to Athens—"Inhale the taste of ancient Greece, boys," he boomed above the traffic choking the Plaka at the foot of the Acropolis.

The Rutherford type—warm, soft heart behind stiff,

unforgiving tweed—has a long ancestry, beloved of journalists, novelists, and playwrights.

As the leading British journalist William Rees-Mogg said in the *Mail on Sunday* in May 2005, talking about his daughter's bid to become Tory MP for Aberavon in Wales, "Country people are not modern, classical schoolmasters are not modern, manufacturers are not modern, particularly if they are involved in heavy industry, the Welsh are not modern. Certainly Aberavon is not modern, and the people suffer because of it."

The classics master is a quick literary shortcut to encapsulating a lonely, highly intelligent man dedicated to his subject, and often to his pupils. They are never in fiction—and rarely in real life—female. They are often dons manqués—men who, due to a personality fault, or an unfortunate incident, never made it as academics. And so they become, like Dr. Rutherford, substitute dons at school, keen on building up one-to-one relationships with the pupils and dismissive of their contemporaries in the school common room.

There was a lot of Rutherford in Andrew Crocker-Harris, "The Crock," in Terence Rattigan's *The Browning Version*, a crusty, short-tempered classics master in a serge suit and a stiff collar, cuckolded by his younger, pretty wife. The crust is broken when a boy gives him Browning's translation of Aeschylus as a present and he bursts into tears:

ANDREW, *left alone, continues for a time staring at the text he has been pretending to read. Then he puts one hand over his eyes. There is a knock on the door.*
ANDREW: Come in.

TAPLOW *appears timidly from behind the screen.*

[*Sharply*] Yes, Taplow? What is it?

TAPLOW: Nothing, sir.

ANDREW: What do you mean, nothing?

TAPLOW: I just came back to say goodbye, sir.

ANDREW: Oh. [*He gets up.*]

TAPLOW: I didn't have a chance with the head here. I rather dashed out, I'm afraid. I thought I'd just come back and—and wish you luck, sir.

ANDREW: Thank you, Taplow. That's good of you.

TAPLOW: I—er—thought this might interest you, sir. [*He quickly thrusts a small book into* ANDREW'S *hand.*]

ANDREW: What is it?

TAPLOW: Verse tranlsation of the *Agamemnon*, sir. *The BrowningVersion.* It's not much good, I've been reading it in the chapel gardens.

ANDREW *very deliberately turns over the pages of the book.*

ANDREW: Very interesting, Taplow. [*He seeems to have a little difficulty in speaking. He clears his throat and then goes on in his level, gentle voice.*] I know the translation, of course. It has its faults, I agree, but I think you will enjoy it more when you get used to the metre he employs.

He hands it to TAPLOW *who brusquely thrusts it back to him.*

TAPLOW: It's for you, sir.

ANDREW: For me?

TAPLOW: Yes, sir. I've written in it.

ANDREW *opens the flyleaf and reads whatever is written there.*

ANDREW: Did you buy this?

TAPLOW: Yes, sir. It was only second-hand.

ANDREW: You shouldn't have spent your pocket-money this way.

TAPLOW: That's all right, sir. It wasn't very much. The price isn't still inside, is it?

ANDREW *carefully wipes his glasses and puts them on again.*

ANDREW: *[at length]* No. Just what you've written. Nothing else.

TAPLOW: Good. I'm sorry you've got it already. I thought you probably would have.

ANDREW: I haven't got it already. I may have had it once. I can't remember. But I haven't got it now.

TAPLOW: That's all right, then.

ANDREW *continues to stare at* TAPLOW'S *inscription on the flyleaf.*

[Suspiciously] What's the matter, sir? Have I got the accent wrong on eimenos?

ANDREW: No. The perispomenon is perfectly correct.

He lowers the book and we notice his hands are shaking from some intense inner effort as he takes off his spectacles.

In Evelyn Waugh's short story "Scott-King's Modern Europe" (1947), Mr. Scott-King, a lonely classics master, makes for the perfect victim of the cruelties of the modern world—"Growing slightly bald and slightly corpulent, known to generations of boys first as 'Scottie,' then of late years, while barely middle-aged, as 'old Scottie'; a school 'institution,' whose precise and slightly nasal lamentations of modern decadence were widely parodied."

After a lifetime of teaching dreary boys way below his intellectual level, he is delighted by what looks like the highlight of his career: an invitation to an obscure Eastern European country, Neutralia, to give a lecture on the obscure poet that he knows more than anyone else in the world about, the seventh-century Latin poet Bellorius.

Scott-King's ultimate disappointment, as he is humiliated and destroyed by the petty, evil ways of his totalitarian hosts, is of a piece with his life, and of a piece with the fictional expectation of all classics masters.

The American classics experience is not so intense but, even there, the caricature exists. In Donna Tartt's *The Secret History*, the classics master is single, obsessive, intellectual, overly devoted to his pupils, fogeyish. His pupils in turn become so devoted to classics that they end up reenacting Bacchic rituals and murdering the class's weak link in the process.

The teacher in the book, Julian Morrow, was in fact based on a real-life teacher of Tartt's, Claude Fredericks, a well-connected bachelor with his own tiny printing operation, the Banyan Press. Born in 1923 and still alive at the time of writing, Fredericks inspired his cleverest pupils—among them Tartt and Roger Kimball, editor of the *New Criterion*—at Bennington in Vermont, the most expensive college in America in the 1980s, forming very close friendships for life, particularly with some of his male students.

The Svengali-like teacher encouraged an otherworldly life devoted to the mind, fine dressing, and fine food. Bret Easton Ellis, another Bennington alumnus, referred to the coterie, and echoed the plot of *The Secret History* in *The Rules of Attraction*—"That weird group of Classics majors stand by, looking like undertakers . . . probably roaming the countryside sacrificing farmers and performing pagan rituals."

For all their devotion to ancient ritual, though, the classics students in *The Secret History* aren't much good at Greek. At one stage, an eighteen-year-old pupil—admittedly the dim murder victim, Bunny Corcoran—says,

"Ablative's the ticket. The hard ones are always ablative."

A slight pause.

"Bunny," said Charles, "you're mixed up. The ablative is in Latin."

"Well, of course, I know that," said Bunny irritably, after a confused pause which seemed to indicate the contrary, "but you know what I mean. Aorist, ablative, all the same thing, really . . ."

Looking back, I now feel the romance that pulses through the thin, dry veins of these devoted classics masters. It is a romance forged from this strange combination—of rigid rules of language coming up against the passionate, orgiastic, murderous history and literature of Italy when Italy was as romantic as it is now, but also happened to rule the world.

A decade of one's youth in dusty classrooms spent rote-learning those clinical rules while, as Dr. Rutherford might have put it, inhaling the bloody, erotic, tragic, funny, distinctly unclinical taste of the ancient world, does not go away.

LATIN TEST

Every now and then, as I said, I am going to throw in a small test of your Latin skills so far, and here I think it would be good to see if you can decline *respublica*—state.

Respublica is declined as two words separated and then joined together, i.e., *res* is declined like *res*, and *publica* like *mensa*. Below is the correct declension. See if you can do it yourself, before turning it upside down to have a peek.

	Singular	Plural
NOM.	respublica	respublicae
VOC.	respublica	respublicae
ACC.	rempublicam	respublicas
GEN.	reipublicae	rerumpublicarum
DAT.	reipublicae	rebuspublicis
ABL.	republica	rebuspublicis

THE GOOD, THE BAD, AND THE OTHER ADJECTIVES

Now, it's time for some pretty relentless tables of adjectives. The annoying thing is that there's no real way round needing to know adjectives. The good thing is, they're pretty easy to learn.

Helpfully, most adjectives go like *dominus* in the masculine, *mensa* in the feminine, and *bellum* in the neuter. Let's start with *bonus, -a, -um* meaning "good."

SINGULAR		
Masculine	**Feminine**	**Neuter**

	Masculine	Feminine	Neuter
NOM.	bonus	bona	bonum
VOC.	bone	bona	bonum
ACC.	bonum	bonam	bonum
GEN.	boni	bonae	boni
DAT.	bono	bonae	bono
ABL.	bono	bona	bono

PLURAL		
Masculine	**Feminine**	**Neuter**

	Masculine	Feminine	Neuter
NOM.	boni	bonae	bona
VOC.	boni	bonae	bona
ACC.	bonos	bonas	bona
GEN.	bonorum	bonarum	bonorum
DAT.	bonis	bonis	bonis
ABL.	bonis	bonis	bonis

First and Second Declension–type adjective

Because of this similarity between adjectives and nouns, Pope Gregory was able to make the world's first bad pun, when he spotted some handsome blond English slaves in the Roman forum:

> "Get those boys over there! Who the bloody hell are they?" asked Pope Gregory.
>
> "Oh those," said a stall-holder, "they're Angles [that is, Englishmen, from *Anglus, -i*]."

"Non Angli [not Englishmen]," said Pope Gregory, barely able to control himself, "sed angeli [but angels]."

By the way, adjectives usually go after the noun they're describing, as in:

> *Ricardus Burtonus ebrius*—A drunk Richard Burton
> (*ebrius,-a, -um adj.*—inebriated).
> Or:
> *Elizabetha Tayloriana bella*—A beautiful Elizabeth
> Taylor

The next lot of adjectives end in *-is* for both masculine and feminine, and *-e* for neuter. An example of an adjective that goes like this is *mirabilis, -is, -e*—wonderful (as in *annus mirabilis*—a wonderful year—an expression used for any year in which a lot of extraordinary things happen). The year of 1809 is the archetypal *annus mirabilis*—the birth year of Tennyson, Gogol, Charles Darwin, Abraham Lincoln, and William Gladstone.

	SINGULAR	
	Masculine/Feminine	Neuter
NOM.	*mirabilis*	*mirabile*
VOC.	*mirabilis*	*mirabile*
ACC.	*mirabilem*	*mirabile*
GEN.	*mirabilis*	*mirabilis*
DAT.	*mirabili*	*mirabili*
ABL.	*mirabili*	*mirabili*

	PLURAL	
	Masculine/Feminine	Neuter
NOM.	*mirabiles*	*mirabilia*
VOC.	*mirabiles*	*mirabilia*
ACC.	*mirabiles*	*mirabilia*
GEN.	*mirabilium*	*mirabilium*
DAT.	*mirabilibus*	*mirabilibus*
ABL.	*mirabilibus*	*mirabilibus*

Third Declension–type adjective

In one of the Queen's wittier moments, she adapted the idiom in 1992 to *annus horribilis*—a bloody terrible year, when Windsor Castle burned down, and the marriages of Prince Charles, Prince Andrew, and Princess Anne fell apart.

The editors at the leading British tabloid, the *Sun*, also showed all the benefits of a classical education during the Christmas of 2005, or MMV, as they'd know to call it.

The Queen had plumped for a serious Christmas broadcast, concentrating on the tsunami of the Christmas before and the Pakistan earthquake that year, and avoiding sugary reminders of Zara Phillips flashing her tongue-stud outside Sandringham Church or any mention of Camilla Parker Bowles. The *Sun* interpreted this as a slight to the new Duchess of Cornwall and so came up with the dream headline SNUBBUS HORRIBILIS. Quite grammatically correct, of course.

It's from the neuter singular nominative of *mirabilis* that we get the saying *mirabile dictu*, i.e., wonderful to say—a phrase to be dropped into conversation liberally, often with heavy-handed irony: "Prince Charles has finally said, *mirabile dictu*, that, after all, it's not too bad living in a London palace and a Gloucestershire country house with half of Cornwall, mortgage-free, to fall back on."

From the same formation, you get *mirabile visu*—wonderful to see, and *horribile dictu*—horrible to say. Also to be used with irony—"*Horribile dictu*, the Delaware guys have seen fit to give me a 200-grand bonus and a company BMW."

There are all sorts of variants on the *mirabilis, -is, -e* form, but they are minor ones. All that really differs is the nominative form and how it changes in the accusative. Once you've got to the genitive, they all pretty much follow *mirabilis*.

So, *celeber*—famous (thus celeb, a rare example of a Latin word shrinking in English, rather than being expanded)—goes to *celebrem* in the accusative and, after that, it's *mirabilis* all over again: *celebris, celebri, celebri*, etc.

That doesn't mean that all adjectives ending in *-er* go like *celeber*. Some, annoyingly, go like *dominus*, e.g., *miser*—miserable, which goes *miser, misera, miserum*.

There's no way of saying which way these adjectives will jump—whether they'll follow *miser* or *celeber*. Your best bet, apart from learning how they all go, is to take a gamble on them going like *miser*, until you gradually become more familiar with the ways of individual words.

Any adjective with an odd-sounding ending, like *felix* or *ingens*, will end up going like *mirabilis*, once it's made the jump to becoming a "fat accusative." So *felix* jumps to *felicem, felicis*, etc., and *ingens* to *ingentem, ingentis*, etc.

COMPARATIVES AND SUPERLATIVES

Now is as good a time as any to deal with these customers, which are nice and easy.

The simple rule of thumb is that if you want to make something "more" whatever, add on *-ior*; and if you want to make it the "mostest" something, add on *-issimus*. So *stultus*—stupid, becomes *stultior*—more stupid, and then becomes *stultissimus*—stupidest.

The same goes for those odder adjectives that sound like Third Declension nouns, i.e., *tristis, -is -e adj.*—sad, which goes *tristior, tristissimus*. As far as declining goes, comparatives go like Third Declension nouns and the superlatives go like *bonus, -a, -um*.

SINGULAR		
	Masculine/Feminine	**Neuter**
NOM.	stultior	stultius
VOC.	stultior	stultius
ACC.	stultiorem	stultius
GEN.	stultioris	stultioris
DAT.	stultiori	stultiori
ABL.	stultiore	stultiore

PLURAL		
	Masculine/Feminine	**Neuter**
NOM.	stultiores	stultiora
VOC.	stultiores	stultiora
ACC.	stultiores	stultiora
GEN.	stultiorum	stultiorum
DAT.	stultioribus	stultioribus
ABL.	stultioribus	stultioribus

Comparative Adjectives—stultior—more stupid

An annoying little irregularity creeps in for *mirabilis*-type words, however. If the Queen were to have an even worse year than 1992, it would be an *annus horribilior*, as you'd imagine. But if she were to have the worst year of all time, she'd double her *l*'s, as it were, and have an *annus horribillimus*.

On the horrid old principle of "the more regularly used,

117

the more irregularly spelled," the adjectives you'll use most take the oddest comparatives and superlatives:

	Masculine	Feminine	Neuter
NOM.	*tristissimus*	*tristissima*	*tristissimum*
VOC.	*tristissime*	*tristissima*	*tristissimum*
ACC.	*tristissimum*	*tristissimam*	*tristissimum*
GEN.	*tristissimi*	*tristissimae*	*tristissimi*
DAT.	*tristissimo*	*tristissimae*	*tristissimo*
ABL.	*tristissimo*	*tristissima*	*tristissimo*
NOM.	*tristissimi*	*tristissimae*	*tristissima*
VOC.	*tristissimi*	*tristissimae*	*tristissima*
ACC.	*tristissimos*	*tristissimas*	*tristissima*
GEN.	*tristissimorum*	*tristissimarum*	*tristissimorum*
DAT.	*tristissimis*	*tristissimis*	*tristissimis*
ABL.	*tristissimis*	*tristissimis*	*tristissimis*

Superlative adjectives: tristissimus—saddest

Bonus—good	*melior*—better	*optimus*—best (thus "optimist")
Malus—bad	*peior*—worse	*pessimus*—worst (thus "pessimist")
Multus—many	*plus*—more	*plurimus*—most

ADVERBS

$\int$tiff drink required for these.

Not much to them, but what there is, is pointlessly compli-cated. To form an adverb from an *-us, -a, -um* style adjective, like *dignus, -a, -um*—worthy, or *tutus, -a, -um*—safe, swap *-e* or *-c* for the *-us*. There's no way of telling which to plump for, except from personal knowledge. So *dignus*—worthy goes to *digne*—worthily, *tutus*—safe to *tuto*—safely, and no one can explain why.

Useful adjectives are inevitably irregular, most strikingly: *bonus*—good goes to *bene*—well. Restaurant Italian—"*Tutto bene, Luigi. Il conto, per favore*"—should help here.

LATIN TEST

In February 2006, it was reported in the *Daily Telegraph* that Ista, a German hip-hop band that raps in Latin, was getting back together after a sudden boom in popularity.

The band was formed a decade ago by seven bored classics pupils at a school in Wilhelmshaven. They roped in their teacher, Edgar Barwig, to make sure the lyrics were in good Latin.

The members of the band have now become architects, teachers, a nurse, and parents, but they got back together after their music came back into vogue.

"Over the years we have sold around two thousand, five hundred CDs," said one band member, Lars Janssen. "Between ten and twenty are bought per month from our Internet site.

"But recently that has doubled and the media interest has been enormous. People have found us over the Internet and we have sold CDs to people in the U.S. and all across Europe. Latin is a good language to rap in actually. It has a good rhythm and can be to the point."

To mark their comeback, the band released a new song—"Caesaris Blues," about being bored in Latin lessons. Their breakthrough track, though, was "Status Quo?" Here it is—see if you can translate it before looking at the translation.

Status Quo?

Radii solis per fenestras
Funduntur; utinam natem
Cum sodalibus, sed—
Hercle! Fallimur.

Nobis praeest blatero, qui
Semper dicat inepta, dum
Impleti simus eius summa
Amentia.

his nonsense.
until we're sick to death of
who keeps saying idiotic things
There's a blithering idiot in charge of us,

bloody Hell, we've messed up.
I wish I could go swimming with my friends but,
Sun rays stream through the window.

VERBAL ABUSE AND THE JOHN CLEESE GUIDE TO LATIN

⟦⟧⟦⟧⟦⟧⟦⟧⟦⟧

Even the brightest people sometimes slip up on the minutiae (from *minutia, -ae, f.*—smallness) of Latin grammar. Just look at clever old John Cleese (Clifton Sports Academy, Downing College, Cambridge) when he played a Roman centurion in *The Life of Brian*:

> BRIAN *approaches the palace to graffiti the wall with an anti-Roman slogan. He begins writing, oblivious to the Roman patrol approaching from behind. The slogan reads* ROMANES EUNT DOMUS.
>
> CENTURION: What's this, then? *ROMANES EUNT DO-MUS?* "People called Romanes they go the house"?
>
> BRIAN: It says "Romans, go home."

CENTURION: No it doesn't. What's Latin for "Roman"?

BRIAN: *(hesitates)*

CENTURION: Come on, come on!

BRIAN: (uncertain) *Romanus.*

CENTURION: Goes like?

BRIAN: *Annus?*

CENTURION: Vocative plural of *annus* is?

BRIAN: *Anni.*

CENTURION: *(takes paintbrush from* BRIAN *and paints over)* "Ro-ma-ni." "Eunt"? What is "eunt"?

BRIAN: "Go."

CENTURION: Conjugate the verb "to go"!

BRIAN: *Ire, eo, is, it, imus, itis, eunt.*

CENTURION: So "eunt" is . . . ?

BRIAN: Third person plural present indicative, "They go."

CENTURION: But "Romans, go home!" is an order, so you must use the . . . ? *(lifts* BRIAN *by his hairs)*

BRIAN: The . . . imperative.

CENTURION: Which is?

BRIAN: Ahm, oh, oh, *I, I!*

CENTURION: How many Romans? *(pulls harder)*

BRIAN: Plural, plural! *Ite.*

CENTURION: *(strikes over* EUNT *and paints* ITE *on the wall)* *(satisfied)* "I-te." "Domus"? Nominative? "Go home," this is motion towards, isn't it, boy?

BRIAN: (*very anxious*) Dative?

CENTURION: *(draws his sword and holds it to* BRIAN'*s throat)*

BRIAN: Ahh! No, ablative, ablative, sir. No, the, accusative, accusative, ah, *domum*, sir.

CENTURION: Except that *domus* takes the . . . ?

BRIAN: . . . the locative, sir!

CENTURION: Which is?

BRIAN: *Domum.*

CENTURION: *(satisfied)* Domum. *(strikes out* DOMUS and writes DOMUM*)* "-*mum.*" Understand?

BRIAN: Yes, sir.

CENTURION: Now write it down a hundred times.

BRIAN: Yes, sir, thank you, sir, hail Caesar, sir.

CENTURION: *(salutes)* Hail Caesar. If it's not done by sunrise, I'll cut your balls off.

Actually John Cleese's centurion wasn't quite right. Yes, *domus* behaves oddly, and yes, "*Romani, ite domum*" is right, but it isn't the locative that Brian used.

The locative is a strange, one-off case, used only when you're "at" or "in" a place. And the locative of *domus*, meaning "at home," is *domi*. Here are the other rules for the locative:

First and Second Declension singular—use the genitive case.

E.g.: *Romae*—in Rome, at Rome

Corinthi—in Corinth, at Corinth

Third Declension singular—use the dative.

E.g.: *Carthagini*—at Carthage, in Carthage

First, Second, and Third Declension plural—use the ablative.

E.g.: *Athenis*—in Athens, at Athens

Sardibus—in Sardes, at Sardes

John Cleese's centurion was mixing up the locative of *domus* with a different rule. With *domus* and *casa* (*casa, -ae, f.*—house), the prepositions *ad*, *ab*, and *in* are not used. The same goes for the names of cities (Rome, Athens, Sparta, etc.) and small islands (Sicily, Crete, etc.). So,

1. Places "to which": name in the accusative without *ad*.
   E.g.: *Romam*—to Rome   *Carthaginem*—to Carthage
   Cretam—to Crete   *Domum*—home, as in Brian's
   "Romans, go home."
2. Places "from which": name in the ablative without *ab*.
   E.g.: *Brundisio*—from   *Athenis*—from Athens
   Brundisium   *Sicilia*—from Sicily

THE "DOS AND DON'TS" OF DOING WORDS — VERBS

Verbs are trickier than adjectives, and just as crucial.

Just to make things even more difficult, nouns *decline* and verbs *conjugate*. To make your head swim a bit more, there are five declensions and four conjugations. But just so you can get a feel for them now, the basic rule is that all verbs in the present tense roughly follow the endings of the most famous verb in Latin, *amo*.

Or, if you want a crude way of remembering a rough version of these endings that makes bored thirteen-year-old boys laugh even halfway through double Latin, remember the vulgarism from earlier—po, piss, pist, pimus, pistis, pants.

With this in mind, you should be able to spot whether any verb is first, second, or third person; singular or plural.

Future and past tenses, which we'll also learn later on, have much the same endings with slightly different roots. I'm just giving you these little pointers on verbs before dealing with them in full, so we can start to do some sentences.

THE GREATEST POEM IN
THE ENGLISH LANGUAGE

The only irregular verb you really need to know inside out is the verb "to be." It's hard to sugarcoat the pill of learning, declining, and conjugating nouns and verbs, particularly one as irregular as "to be." The closest thing to sugar I can find is some old TV footage of a drunk Richard Burton, squeezed into a far-too-tight red polo neck, spending his declining years conjugating his favorite verb.

"The greatest poem in the English language," he said, "is the verb 'to be.' I AM [long pause], you ARE [longer pause], he, she, or it IS, we ARE, you ARE, they ARE."

I think his point was that this rote conjugation had a

sort of beauty to it, as an affirmation of life. Either way, you can con yourself into thinking the same about Latin conjugation in general and there certainly is a poetry to conjugating if you do it quickly enough. Try saying, "*Sum, es, est, sumus, estis, sunt*" as quickly as possible and it begins to stick in your mind as a little poem to be enjoyed rather than a list to be learned.

You may recall the phrase "*Civis Romanus sum*" ("I am a Roman citizen"), which became famous in 1850 when Lord Palmerston sent British ships to Athens to settle the claims of Don Pacifico, a Jew from Gibraltar and a British subject, whose house had been damaged by the Greeks.

Palmerston said at the time, "As the Roman, in days of old, held himself free from indignity when he could say, '*Civis Romanus Sum*,' so also a British subject in whatever land he may be, shall feel confident that the watchful eye and the strong arm of England will protect him against injustice and wrong."

Apart from the verb "to be," you needn't learn the irregular verbs and nouns yet. The simple principle to remember is the one we've already come across: the more regularly used, the more irregularly spelled. This is because, so experts think, the more familiar words have been warped by overuse.

YOUR FIRST SENTENCE

Ricardus Burtonus suam uxorem Elizabetham Taylorianam amavit.
Richard Burton loved his wife, Elizabeth Taylor.

Elizabetha Tayloriana Ricardum virum suum deseruit.
Elizabeth Taylor left her husband, Richard.

VOCAB.

uxor, -oris, f.—a wife
amo, amare, amavi, amatum—I love
desero, -ere, -ui, desertum—I desert
suus, -a, -um, adj.—his, her, their own
vir, viri, m.—a man, husband

Now to deal properly with verbs. Deep breath time again. As I said, there are four conjugations of verbs. The way to sum up a verb is in its so-called principal parts, that is, the four familiar forms of each verb.

So, with *amo*, the principal parts are: *amo, amare, amavi, amatum*—"I love," "to love," "I have loved," and the so-called supine.

Thus in any Latin dictionary, the principal parts of a verb are laid out next to its definition, to show the four basic forms that you'll come across: i.e., *facio, facere, feci, factum*—"I do/make."

The first principal part is the most simple form of the verb, the first person (that is, "I . . .") singular present. This always ends in -o: *exsudo*—"I sweat/exude"; *turpo*—"I make ugly/defile."

Incidentally, a good way to remember the spelling of the adjective "principal" (as opposed to the noun, "principle") is the fact that the Latin adjective meaning "leading," from *princeps, -ipis m.*—prince, is *principalis, -e*. (By the way, when I list only two genders, like here with *principalis, -e*, that's because it goes the same in both the masculine and the feminine.)

The second principal part is the infinitive (i.e., "to stroke," "to fiddle," etc.). This always ends with -*re*, but the letter before the -*re* changes according to the conjugation.

> *amo, amare*—to love (first conjugation)
>
> *moneo, monere*—to warn (second conjugation)
>
> *rego, regere*—to rule (third conjugation)
>
> *audio, audire*—to hear (fourth conjugation)

You can use the infinitive as a noun, and the noun is always neuter. So, *Errare est humanum, ignosci divinum*—"To err is human, to forgive divine" (Alexander Pope). English pedants date their dislike of a split infinitive from Latin. Since you can't split a Latin infinitive because it's a single word, you shouldn't do it in English, or so the pedants say.

That seems bloody stupid to me—Latin and English are two different languages.

"To boldly go where no man has gone before" (Captain Kirk, *Starship Enterprise Logbook*) actually sounds better than

"Boldly to go . . ." or "To go boldly . . . ," and is easily translated into Latin—"*Ire audacter eo quo nemo antea.*"

The principal parts of *eo*—"I go," are, by the way, a nightmare: *eo, ire, ii, itum.* Incidentally, the English "ire" has nothing to do with *ire*—"to go," and everything to do with *ira, irae f.*—anger.

EVERETT COLLECTIONS

Their mission? To boldly split infinitives.

To form the perfect infinitive, you take the perfect stem—
say, *lacrimavi*—"I have cried"—and add on *-sse* at the end:

Better to have loved and lost than never to have
loved at all.
*Amavisse et amisisse mallem quam omnino non
amavisse.*

VOCAB.
amitto, -mittere, -misi, -missum—I lose
malo, malle, malui—I wish
omnino—altogether

The third principal part is the perfect tense:

> *amo, amare, amavi*
>
> *moneo, monere, monui*
>
> *rego, regere, rexi*
>
> *audio, audire, audivi*

And the fourth principal part is the supine, which
doesn't have an English equivalent. It is formed from the past
participle of the verb in its nominative, neuter form.

The past participle is a wonderfully useful little device,
because it converts the verb into an adjective: *amatus*—
"beloved," *lacrimatus*—"wept over," *necatus*—"murdered," *fatiga-
tus*—"tired."

N.B. There'll be more about the past participle later.

Cynthia prima suis miserum me cepit ocellis, contactum nullis ante cupidinibus.

Cynthia first trapped me with her little eyes, miserable old me who hadn't been touched [*contactum*—past participle] by desire before.

Propertius, *Elegies I*, Cynthia

VOCAB.

capio, capere, cepi, captum—I capture

ocellus, -i m.—a little eye (diminutive of *oculus, -i, m.*—eye)

contingo, contingere, contigi, contactum—I touch

cupido, -idinis, f.—desire (as in Cupid)

So the supine always ends in *-um* and has mildly differing forms in the different conjugations:

> *amo, amare, amavi, amatum*
>
> *moneo, monere, monui, monitum*
>
> *rego, regere, rexi, rectum*
>
> *audio, audire, audivi, auditum*

Note, too, that the supine is the fertile source for English-related words: amatory, monitor, auditory . . .

Arnold Schwarzenegger was wrongly christened the Governator when he became the governor of California in 2003. He should have been called the Gubernator, the Roman for governor, the man who would govern a province. It comes from *guberno, -are, -avi, -atum*. In the same way, the Terminator comes from *termino, -are, -avi, -atum*—I end.

There's no need to learn all the conjugations by heart, yet, but just be aware that there are four of them and that they all have slightly different roots. Just for completeness's sake, though, here are all the four present tenses of the four conjugations:

1. amo—I love
amas—you (s.) love
amat—he/she/it loves
amamus—we love
amatis—you (pl.) love
amant—they love

2. moneo—I warn
mones—you (s.) warn
monet—he/she/it warns
monemus—we warn
monetis—you (pl.) warn
monent—they warn

3. rego—I rule
regis—you (s.) rule
regit—he/she/it rules
regimus—we rule
regitis—you (pl.) rule
regunt—they rule

4. audio—I hear
audis—you (s.) hear
audit—he/she/it hears
audimus—we hear
auditis—you (pl.) hear
audiunt—they hear

For the hundreds of years that Latin has been taught in English and American schools, "Amo, *amas, amat . . .*" has been the subject's iconic cry. As the basis for learning the simplest form of verb and one of the most crucial—"I love"—it still holds that iconic power.

Eugenie Howard-Johnston, a twenty-five-year-old graduate of Cheltenham Ladies' College (an elite British girls' school) and New College, Oxford, who cuts a fetching figure in scrunched-up hair and boho jangly-jewelry-meets-Dad's-V-neck, teaches Latin at St. Saviour's and St. Olave's, a tough school in Elephant and Castle, a poor area of south London.

Miss Howard-Johnston—or Miss Ho-Jo, as her pupils like to call her—teaches Latin by rapping in the language, and rapping surprisingly well, too. (And there, buried away two thirds through the rap, is the old cry heard through the grandest schools in the land for centuries—*amo, amas, amat* . . .):

> In urbano jungle of SE1
> Leo lays aside suum gun,
> Walks on stage portans his Latin book,
> Turns to page unam, has a brief look,
> Shuts id iterum, begins to clap,
> Stamps his pedes et starts his rap:
> "Odi et amo—that's how it goes
> A hater and a lover and I guess it shows:
> Ego everyday in urbe fight
> Tum turn to find some amorem at night.
> Cur tu stand there looking so yellow?
> Num tu afraid that ego bellum gero?
> No! Pacem quaero—and yeah it's cheesy
> Sed tibi dico, that it ain't easy."
> He turns around and ridet at his mum,
> She smiles back while the canes hum.
> "Amo, amas, amat," they whisper in time

As Leo continues with his rhyme.
"Amamus, amatis, and amant,"
The canes sing as the descant.
The lights go down, the cives applaud—
"Leo!" clamant, "tu es noster Latin Lord!"

PRONOUNS

Pronouns are tricky, fiddly things to learn, partly because they all sound so similar—*is, ea, id, ipse, ille etc*—but they're pretty crucial.

Me, Me, Me

An unsurprisingly well-used word in Latin is "me" or more correctly "I"—or *ego*, as it is in Latin. This goes:

	Singular	**Plural**
NOM.	*Ego*	*Nos*
ACC.	*Me*	*Nos*
GEN.	*Mei*	*Nostri/Nostrum*
DAT.	*Mihi*	*Nobis*
ABL.	*Me*	*Nobis*

Incidentally, a 'nostrum" is a medicine or a scheme promising all sorts of cures, with no demonstrable value. In one of the examples of how a derivation can get unrecognizably warped from its original meaning, the word comes from the cry of the medicine-seller, "*Nostrum, nostrum*"—"Ours, ours (. . . come get our quack remedy, our answer to the crisis in the Middle East, our secret of true love, etc.)."

By the way, my prep school magazine had the rather brilliant name of *Nobis*. Showing the great flexibility of Latin, *nobis*, in the dative and ablative, means "to us, for us, by, with, and from us."

You, *tu*, goes:

	Singular	**Plural**
NOM.	*Tu*	*Vos*
ACC.	*Te*	*Vos*
GEN.	*Tui*	*Vestri/Vestrum*
DAT.	*Tibi*	*Vobis*
ABL.	*Te*	*Vobis*

Being Self-ish

While in English we have the nice, lazy device of adding on "self" to a pronoun to add emphasis and make what is called a reflexive pronoun, the Romans had different words for each self.

"Himself," "herself," or "itself" are all translated into *se*, as in "per se" ("in and of itself").

Helpfully, there is no plural form for *se*—i.e., you use *se* to mean "themselves" as well as "himself/itself/herself." And there is no nominative of *se*, because, as it were, somebody can only do something to himself as an object.

There is no separate word for "myself "; it is covered by *ego*, as above—*me*.

ACC.	*Se*—himself, herself, itself, or themselves
GEN.	*Sui*—of himself
DAT.	*Sibi*—to himself
ABL.	*Se*—by, with, or from himself

THE FUTURE TENSE

To put it simply, first and second conjugation verbs like *amo* and *moneo* throw in a "b" for the future; third and fourth ones like *rego* and *audio* throw in an "e" in their roots:

> **1.** *amabo*—I will love
> *amabis*—you (s.) will love
> *amabit*—he/she/it will love
> *amabimus*—we will love
> *amabitis*—you (pl.) will love
> *amabunt*—they will love

> **2.** *monebo*—I will warn
> *monebis*—you (s.) will warn
> *monebit*—he/she/it will warn
> *monebimus*—we will warn
> *monebitis*—you (pl.) will warn
> *monebunt*—they will warn

3. *regam*—I will rule
   reges—you (s.) will rule
   reget—he/she/it will rule
   regemus—we will rule
   regetis—you (pl.) will rule
   regent—they will rule

4. *audiam*—I will hear
   audies—you (s.) will hear
   audiet—he/she/it will hear
   audiemus—we will hear
   audietis—you (pl.) will hear
   audient—they will hear

THE IMPERFECT TENSE

This means the tense "I was tittering/weeping/raking." It's an easy one to do because it's much the same through the conjugations. All you have to do is add on *-bam* at the end of each verb and then conjugate pretty much as normal.

1. *amabam*—I was loving
   amabas—you (s.) were loving
   amabat—he/she/it was loving
   amabamus—we were loving
   amabatis—you (pl.) were loving
   amabant—they were loving

2. *monebam*—I was warning
   monebas—you (s.) were warning
   monebat—he/she/it was warning
   monebamus—we were warning
   monebatis—you (pl.) were warning
   monebant—they were warning

3. *regebam*—I was ruling
   regebas—you (s.) were ruling
   regebat—he/she/it was ruling
   regebamus—we were ruling
   regebatis—you (pl.) were ruling
   regebant—they were ruling

4. *audiebam*—I was hearing
   audiebas—you (s.) were hearing
   audiebat—he/she/it was hearing
   audiebamus—we were hearing
   audiebatis—you (pl.) were hearing
   audiebant—they were hearing

THE PERFECT TENSE

The best-known three perfect tenses in Latin are the ones on the top of Caesar's CV (short for "curriculum vitae," literally "the running order of life"; curriculum comes from *curro, currere, cucurri, cursum*—I run): *Veni, vidi, vici*—"I came, I saw, I conquered" (as Caesar said when he defeated Pharnaces, King of Pontus, in one day at the Battle of Zela in 47 BC).

Actually, the perfect is wrongly named. It's certainly not perfectly easy to learn, nor is it perfectly formed.

But then our use of the word "perfect" is different to the original Latin use of the word. The word "perfect" comes from *perficio, perficere, perfeci, perfectum*—I do thoroughly. So *perfectus* means "having been done thoroughly."

This is as opposed to the imperfect, which means an ongoing act in the past that hasn't been completed: i.e., imperfect— "I was kissing her, when her enormous brother Sid turned up"; perfect—"I kissed her, and then told her that I was more attracted to her enormous brother Sid."

There are two ways of translating the perfect: "I broiled" or "I have broiled."

The second sense must be relied upon for the cleverest show-off joke in the history of the British Empire, made by Sir Charles Napier, the nineteenth-century general. (It was Sir Charles's statue in Trafalgar Square that the Mayor of London, Ken Livingstone, took against so vehemently in October 2000 because he thought Napier was an outdated colonial.)

Charged with fighting for and occupying the Indian city of Miani in the province of Sind in northwest India in 1843, Sir Charles pulled it off nice and quickly. His telegram back to the Indian Office was nice and quick, too. "*Peccavi*" is all he wrote, i.e., "I have sinned," from *pecco, peccare, peccavi, peccatum*— "I sin." Get it?

Anyway, the joke depends on some clever classicist be-ing around in the Indian Office on the day the telegram arrived; a classicist so clever that he knew to translate it as "I have sinned" as opposed to "I sinned," which wouldn't have made much sense to Lord Palmerston in Downing Street at the time.

The perfect tense has all sorts of irregular endings, varies greatly across the conjugations, and is the point where verbs have a sort of nervous breakdown and go into meltdown. That melted-down form is, annoyingly, where some of the related nouns are drawn from.

So *rego*—I rule, goes *rego, regere, rexi, rectum*. Because the noun comes from the perfect, the Latin for "ruler" or "king" is then not *reg*, but *rex*. So here are the four conjugations.

1. *amavi*—I have loved
   amavisti—you (s.) have loved
   amavit—he/she/it has loved
   amavimus—we have loved
   amavistis—you have loved
   amaverunt—they have loved

2. *monui*—I have warned
   monuisti—you (s.) have warned
   monuit—he/she/it has warned
   monuimus—we have warned
   monuistis—you (pl.) have warned
   monuerunt—they have warned

3. *rexi*—I have ruled
rexisti—you (s.) have ruled
rexit—he/she/it has ruled
reximus—we have ruled
rexistis—you (pl.) have ruled
rexerunt—they have ruled

4. *audivi*—I have heard
audivisti—you (s.) have heard
audivit—he/she/it has heard
audivimus—we have heard
audivistis—you (pl.) have heard
audiverunt—they have heard

THE PLUPERFECT TENSE

The pluperfect—literally, plusperfect—means "more perfect" or, if you like, "even more completed," i.e., further back in time. So you translate the pluperfect—"I had snuffled/necked/ smooched."

Some consolation of going through all the rigmarole of learning the perfect means that the pluperfect becomes a cinch. All you do is take the perfect root above, and add in:

-eram

-eras

-erat

-eramus

-eratis

-erant

So the four conjugations go:

1. *amaveram*—I had loved
   amaveras—you (s.) had loved
   amaverat—he/she/it had loved
   amaveramus—we had loved
   amaveratis—you (pl.) had loved
   amaverant—they had loved

2. *monueram*—I had warned
   monueras—you (s.) had warned
   monuerat—he/she/it had warned
   monueramus—we had warned
   monueratis—you (pl.) had warned
   monuerant—they had warned

3. *rexeram*—I had ruled
   rexeras—you (s.) had ruled
   rexerat—he/she/it had ruled
   rexeramus—we had ruled
   rexeratis—you (pl.) had ruled
   rexerant—they had ruled

4. *audiveram*—I had heard
   audiveras—you (s.) had heard
   audiverat—he/she/it had heard

audiveramus—we had heard
audiveratis—you (pl.) had heard
audiverant—they had heard

ORDERING SOMEONE ABOUT—THE IMPERATIVE

When you tell someone to do something directly—"Wash your mouth out with soap," "Bury him before *rigor mortis* ('the stiffness of death,' by the way) sets in"—you use the imperative.

Although in English we use only one sort of imperative, whether we're telling a six-month-old baby to go to sleep or, over a PA, telling 60,000 Yankees fans not to smoke in the stadium, the Romans had a singular and a plural imperative.

The comforting thing, though, is that the imperative is very simple and, fittingly, curt. For the singular imperative for *amo, moneo,* and *audio,* all you do is take the root, *ama, mone,* and *audi* (like the car)—and that's it. So, "Love her" is "*Ama eam.*" "Show the picture" is "*Monstra imaginem.*"

The plural is easy, too—just add *-te* on to the singular:

Tell Laura I love her (addressed to one person).
Narra Laurae me eam amare.
Tell Laura I love her (addressed to more than one person).
Narrate Laurae me eam amare.

AILSA MAINWARING

Postmen of Pompeii, you have been warned

Rego is predictably difficult, going *rege* in the singular, but *regite* in the plural.

A famous Second Declension imperative is "*Cave canem*"—"Beware of the dog."

PARTICIPLES

Participles are what you make when you turn a noun into an adjective, i.e., "the 'running' boy," "the 'kissing' gate," "the 'mass-murdering' grandmother." In the present tense, they're formed by adding on -*ans*, -*ens*, or whatever the root might be to the verb. So the classic conjugations are *amans, monens, regens, audiens*. They all decline like Third Declension adjectives:

	Masculine & Feminine		Neuter	
	Singular	**Plural**	**Singular**	**Plural**
NOM.	*amans*	*amantes*	*amans*	*amantia*
VOC.	*amans*	*amantes*	*amans*	*amantia*
ACC.	*amantem*	*amantes*	*amans*	*amantia*
GEN.	*amantis*	*amantium*	*amantis*	*amantium*
DAT.	*amanti*	*amantibus*	*amanti*	*amantibus*
ABL.	*amanti*	*amantibus*	*amanti*	*amantibus*

The present participle of amo

There's a perfect participle, too, which is, basically, formed by adding on -*tus* to the verb's root. This, in the neuter, is the same as the supine—the last principal part of the verb, which we met earlier: *amatum, monitum, rectum, auditum*.

So . . . *amatus, monitus, rectus, auditus*—"having been loved," "having been advised," "having been ruled," "having been heard"—all decline like *dominus* in the masculine, *mensa* in the feminine, and *bellum* in the neuter:

> *amatus, -a, -um*
>
> *monitus, -a, -um*
>
> *rectus, -a, -um*
>
> *auditus, -a, -um*

There is also a very odd-looking future participle. This is made by taking the perfect participle stem, *amat-, monit-*, etc., and adding on *-urus, -ura, -urum*, depending on the case:

> *amaturus, -a, -um*
>
> *moniturus, -a, -um*
>
> *recturus, -a, -um*
>
> *auditurus, -a, -um*

The future participle is a marvelously versatile, compact thing. It can mean "about to do . . . ," "on the verge of doing . . . ," "just before doing . . . ," e.g.,

Mittus Romnus, Hillariam Clintonam victurus, se pharmaca potentissima cotidie consumere admisit.

Just when he was about to beat Hillary Clinton [from *vinco, vincere, vici, victum*—I conquer], Mitt Romney admitted to a severe Class-A drug habit.

BOTANISTS' LATIN

If you're short of laughs, take a walk round a country house garden this afternoon, and look for the Women's Institute Walk. The Women's Institute is the local social club for ladies across Britain. You'll know what I mean when you see the walk: a group of women in middle-to-late-middle age, walking as slowly as possible without actually stopping.

And then they do stop, as they pass an obscure-looking plant. Gently pointing at the plant, they start to make a very particular tribal cry, distinguished by a series of tentative questions, disguising huge confidence and great doses of one-upmanship. And a lot of Latin.

"What sort of foxglove is that?"

"*Scrophulariaceae.*"

"Yes, I know that. But what's the species?"

"*Digitalis.*"

"Yes, but what sort?"

"*Digitalis lutea,* isn't it?"

"Isn't that the yellow one?"

"Of course it is. Silly me. That's *digitalis purpurea.* They're all over the hedgerows on the Woodstock road from Oxford."

To get over this showing off, you may be tempted to go to the nearest National Trust café and drink as much Audley End Elderflower Wine or Waddesdon Home Brew as they've got in stock.

Or you might want to learn how to do the W.I. Walk and War Cry yourself. It's actually very easy and it makes a lot of sense.

Different countries and different regions of each country develop different words for the same plant: a Scottish bluebell is a harebell in England and Wales. So it's logical to have a common name for each plant, and, given the shared Latin root to most European languages, it's logical that the name is in Latin.

A Peruvian botanist will no doubt stare off, nonplussed, in the direction of the Andes if you start talking about daffodils. Say narcissus and you'll have his undivided attention.

Plants with lots of features in common can be divided up into species, genus, and family. The species (the plural, nice and confusingly, is also species) are the tightest little groups, normally found in the same area. They don't tend to interbreed, although they can; witness the victory of the coarse Spanish bluebell over the delicate English one.

If the species have enough characteristics in common, they are grouped together into a genus (plural, genera). And genera with features in common are called families, like orchids or bamboo.

So, in the W.I. War Cry above, *Scrophulariaceae* is the plant family name. *Digitalis*, meaning foxglove, is the genus name. And *Digitalis lutea* (yellow foxglove) or *Digitalis purpurea* (purple foxglove) is the species name.

Here are some words used to classify different species:

nigrum—black, *alba*—white, *gigantium*—large, *cespitosa*—tufted, *foetidissima*—horrible smelling, *maritime*—found by the sea, *Cambricum*—Welsh, *Americanus*—natural to America, *Canadensis*—natural to Canada, *officinale*—medicinal.

To get an A in the W.I. War Cry, you can learn the even more precise classifications. The prefix "ssp." before the species name means "*subspecies*," i.e., another group within the species group.

If the species name has "var."(short for "variety") in front of it, that means the plant is a naturally occurring mutation that a gardener has deliberately propagated.

If the Latin name has an English proper name or a descriptive name after it, say *Daphne bholua "Winfrey"* or *Rosa azura "Blues in the Night,"* then it's a garden cultivar. That means it's a plant that's been cultivated for color, smell, or foliage, and given a special name by its cultivator to sum up its special quality or to show the cultivator's reverence for his favorite talk show hostess from Chicago.

Incidentally, much the same system applies to animals, as Jeeves points out to Bertie Wooster in *Right Ho, Jeeves* (1934):

> "You must have heard of newts. Those little sort of lizard things that charge around in ponds."
> "Oh, yes, sir. The aquatic members of the family Salamandridae which constitute the species Molge."

ACTIVE AND PASSIVE

These words may sound scary, but they're simple enough.

An active verb is exactly that—it means acting, doing something to somebody else. A passive verb means exactly that, too—i.e., doing nothing and having something done to oneself. So if you are "being thwacked," "are about to be flogged," or "have been bullied," then you're in the passive.

A rough rule of thumb is to look for an *-r* at the end of a verb if you're on the lookout for a passive. Here's how they go:

> **1.** *amor*—I am loved
> *amaris*—you (s.) are loved
> *amatur*—he/she/it is loved
> *amamur*—we are loved
> *amamini*—you (pl.) are loved
> *amantur*—they are loved

> **2.** *moneor*—I am warned
> *moneris*—you (s.) are warned
> *monetur*—he/she/it is warned
> *monemur*—we are warned
> *monemini*—you (pl.) are warned
> *monentur*—they are warned

> **3.** *regor*—I am ruled
> *regeris*—you (s.) are ruled

regitur—he/she/it is ruled
regimur—we are ruled
regimini—you (pl.) are ruled
reguntur—they are ruled

4. *audior*—I am heard
audiris—you (s.) are heard
auditur—he/she/it is heard
audimur—we are heard
audimini—you (pl.) are heard
audiuntur—they are heard

DEPONENT

An annoying little wrinkle on the passive is that some verbs that decline like passive verbs turn out to be active.

These are called deponent verbs and their futures, imperfects, perfects, etc. all go like future passives, imperfect passives, etc. Even more annoyingly, they're quite common. Among the ones you'll regularly bump into are:

> *Hortor, hortari, hortatus sum*—I encourage
> *Loquor, loqui, locutus sum*—I speak (thus "eloquent," "loquacious")
> *Reor, reri, ratus sum*—I think (thus "rational")
> *Sequor, sequi, secutus sum*—I follow (thus "sequence")

Nascor, nasci, natus sum—I am born (thus "pre/ postnatal")

Patior, pati, passus sum—I suffer (thus the "passive" voice, as opposed to the "active" voice, which comes from *ago, agere, egi, actum*—"I do")

One of the useful things about the deponent is that its past participle is active—i.e., it can take an object—not passive, like other verbs. That means you can use the deponent past participle in a much freer way than the passive past participles: "Having suffered life, he loved death," is just "*Vitam passus, mortem amavit.*"

But if you wanted to say, "Once he'd made his bed and brushed his teeth, he killed himself," you'd have to make everything clumsier by turning each little clause into the so-called ablative absolute—"The bed having been made, the teeth having been brushed . . .": "*Lecto formato, dentibus versatis, se occidit.*"

VOCAB.

lectus, -i m.—bed
formo, -are—I form, shape
dens, dentis m.—a tooth
verro, verrere, verri, versum—I brush, scour
occido, -ere, occidi, occisum—I kill

THE ABLATIVE ABSOLUTE

If the words "ablative absolute" send the spirits plunging, better to think of it as the "while" word. In other words, if you think of an expression with two things going on at the same time, the "while" bit is an ablative absolute.

> Suave, mari magno turbantibus aequora ventis,
> E terra magnum alterius spectare laborem.

> How lovely it is to gaze from the shore at somebody having a terrible time, while the wind whips up the waters on the huge sea.

Lucretius, On the Nature of Things, The Epicurean Ideal—Peace of Mind

For an ablative absolute, you put both the noun in the ablative and the verb in the ablative of the participle form. "Te dormiente . . ." "With you sleeping . . ."

However, you need to be on your guard when translating ablative absolutes. It is most important to try to steer clear of the "with the legionary bearing malice to the ditches, the Gaul assaulted him" school of heavy-handed Latin.

FUTURE PASSIVE

The future passive is a funny little hybrid of the future active with similar endings to the present passive. A bit of a nightmare to learn.

1. *amabor*—I will be loved
   amaberis—you (s.) will be loved
   amabitur—he/she/it will be loved
   amabimur—we will be loved
   amabimini—you (pl.) will be loved
   amabuntur—they will be loved

2. *monebor*—I will be warned
   moneberis—you (s.) will be warned
   monebitur—he/she/it will be warned
   monebimur—we will be warned
   monebimini—you (pl.) will be warned
   monebuntur—they will be warned

3. *regar*—I will be ruled
   regeris—you (s.) will be ruled
   regetur—he/she/it will be ruled
   regemur—we will be ruled
   regemini—you (pl.) will be ruled
   regentur—they will be ruled

4. *audiar*—I will be heard
audieris—you (s.) will be heard
audietur—he/she/it will be heard
audiemur—we will be heard
audiemini—you (pl.) will be heard
audientur—they will be heard

PERFECT PASSIVE

The perfect passive is easy as pie. All you do is take the perfect participle and add on the verb "to be" at the end. So "I have been loved/shown/ruled/heard" goes: *Amatus/monitus/ rectus/auditus sum*. And so it goes on:

Amatus/monitus/rectus/auditus sum
Amatus/monitus/rectus/auditus es
Amatus/monitus/rectus/auditus est
Amatus/monitus/rectus/auditus sumus
Amatus/monitus/rectus/auditus estis
Amatus/monitus/rectus/auditus sunt

1,484 YEARS OF PURPLE TOGAS— OR ROMAN EMPERORS AND THEIR GREATEST HITS

᠊᠊᠊᠊᠊᠊

P hew. That was quite heavy going, so I think it's time for a brief digression on Roman emperors. There's no need to learn them all, though. There are far too many of them who did nothing of interest. But here's a list of the notable ones—with important juicy facts added where needed.

Augustus was the first Roman emperor. He invented the job in 31 BC after centuries of the Roman Republic, which had lasted since the expulsion from Rome of the last Tarquinian king, Tarquinius Superbus, in 510 BC.

Before Augustus made himself emperor, there had been two triumvirates (from *tres* and *viri*—three men) in charge: 60–54 BC—Caesar, Pompey, and Crassus; 43–33 BC—Octavian (as Augustus was originally called), Lepidus, and Mark Antony.

Augustus took up the surname Caesar in honor of Julius, his great-uncle. All Augustus's successors then took on the name Caesar, too, accruing the same sort of Brownie points that the British royal family got by ditching the surname Saxe-Coburg-Gotha and going for "Windsor" instead.

The Germans and the Russians also took on the name Caesar in later centuries in the form of Kaisers and Tsars.

You might be interested to know that Julius Caesar was offered the title of king but turned it down three times. He was happy enough wearing purple and being dictator, and being deified in 42 BC, two years after he was murdered by Brutus and Cassius. (Emperors took to wearing purple, partly because it was such a difficult dye to get hold of—it cost more, ounce for ounce, than gold. Ten thousand Murex molluscs had to be crushed to produce enough dye for one "toga picta"—painted toga.)

Anyway, here goes:

31 BC–AD 14: Augustus—He ended a century of civil war in Rome and, as he said in his show-off autobiography, *Res Gestae—The Things I've Done* (literally, "The Things Done")—"I found Rome a city of brick and made it marble."

The month of August (Latin *Augustus*) is named after Augustus; before it had been called *Sextilis* (the sixth month of the Roman calendar). August has 31 days because Augustus wanted his month to be as long as Julius Caesar's July.

Augustus set in place the so-called Pax Romana for the next two hundred years (notwithstanding minor scraps with the British and half of Europe). He began the expansion of the empire, which over the next two centuries saw it spread its boundaries to Armenia, Mesopotamia, the Arabian desert, the Red Sea, Nubia, the Sahara, the Moroccan mountains, the Atlantic Ocean, the Irish Sea, Scotland, the North Sea, the Rhine, the Danube, the Black Sea, and the Caucasus.

AD 14–37: Tiberius—Augustus's stepson, who spent the last decade of his life in his clifftop palace in Capri, occasionally hurling enemies into the sea.

Made the mistake of getting too pally with a minion, Sejanus, head of the elite, and presumably crack, Praetorian Guard. Sejanus, when in Tiberius's favor, assumed semi-imperial powers. Once he was out of the emperor's favor, the Praetorian Guard turned on Sejanus and executed him.

AD 37–41: Gaius (Caligula)—Neither quite as wet as John Hurt's portrayal of him in *I, Claudius*, nor as sexually depraved as Malcolm McDowell is in Gore Vidal's 1979 film *Caligula*.

Certainly spoilt, possibly mad: got so close to his favorite racehorse, Incitatus, that he invited guests to dinner in Incitatus's name, and even considered making Incitatus a consul.

Caligula means "Little Boot," and was derived from his childhood in a Roman army camp, where he wore a miniature soldier's costume.

◧◧◧◧◧

AD 41–54: Claudius—As in "I," the stuttering emperor played by Derek Jacobi in the 1977 series.

Certainly scholarly, as depicted in the series, he also had a cruel streak, with an addiction to watching gladiators kill each other. Liked to watch his defeated opponents being executed.

But, on the plus side, Claudius did lead the second invasion of Britain in AD 43, after Julius Caesar's first go (see Roman Britain, *infra*). Claudius was so keen on the British that he even called his son, born in AD 41—i.e., before the invasion—Britannicus.

Sadly, though, Claudius wasn't so keen on the boy and we missed out on the pleasure of an Emperor Britannicus. Instead the purple toga went to Claudius's adopted son Nero.

◧◧◧◧◧

AD 54–68: Nero—Not quite true that he fiddled while Rome burned. Certainly he had "artistic leanings"—although he was vigorously heterosexual, with two wives, Octavia and Poppaea—and took to appearing on stage and singing in public.

When a huge fire left most of Rome in ashes in AD 64, he did little to help rebuild the city and some suspected he lit the fires himself.

Nero did, though, build himself an elaborate, beautifully frescoed palace, the *Domus Aurea*, or Golden House. This selfishness, combined with his taste for singing, stoked the fiddling myth.

There were then various nonentities:

AD 68–69: Galba

AD 69: Otho

AD 69: Vitellius

AD 69–79: Vespasian, who began building the Colosseum

AD 79–81: Titus, who finished building it

AD 81–96: Domitian

AD 96–98: Nerva

Until:

AD 98–117: Trajan—Perhaps the greatest show-off of them all, with the erection of Trajan's Column recording his triumph over the Dacians of modern Romania in AD 101–102 and 105–106.

On the friezes that wrap their way all around the column in the middle of Trajan's forum in Rome, the emperor is always shown as taller than other Romans, and much taller than the Dacians.

⊡⊡⊡⊡⊡

AD 117–138: Hadrian—As in the wall, seventy-three and a half miles long, six feet high, eight feet thick, stretching from Wallsend on the Tyne, in the east, to Bowness at the head of Solway Firth, in the west, roughly dividing England from Scotland.

⊡⊡⊡⊡⊡

AD 138–161: Antoninus Pius—Who, with his successor, Marcus Aurelius, set up the so-called Golden Age of the Roman Empire, the calm before the storm.

⊡⊡⊡⊡⊡

AD 161–180: Marcus Aurelius—The cleverest of the Roman emperors, whose *Meditations* are still in print.

Very avant-garde: "You will give yourself relief, if you do every act of your life as if it were the last, laying aside all carelessness and passionate aversion from the commands of reason, and all hypocrisy, and self-love, and discontent with the portion which has been given to you" (*Meditations* II.V).

⊡⊡⊡⊡⊡

AD 180–192: Commodus—According to Edward Gibbon in *The History of the Decline and Fall of the Roman Empire*, "If a man were called to fix the period in the history of the world, during which the condition of the human race was most happy and prosperous, he would, without hesitation, name that which elapsed from the death of Domitian to the accession of Commodus."

With Commodus came the decline of the Roman Empire as the Praetorian Guard started to muscle in on the emperors' act.

Between AD 192 and 306 there are plenty of emperors, but none that you will need to bother your head about, although if you want to show off, you could drop a Diadumenianus or an Elagabalus into conversation.

AD 306–337: Constantine I—Changed the world by converting to Christianity on his deathbed. This epoch-making decision grew out of the victory over Maxentius at the Battle of Milvian Bridge, outside Rome, in AD 312.

The night before battle, Constantine saw the two Greek letters Chi and Rho, the symbol of Christ, shining above the sun. He had his soldiers paint the symbol on their shields and, following his victory, he started considering his conversion.

He then went on to transfer the capital of the Roman Empire from Rome to the ancient city of Byzantium, re-named Constantinople, later to become Istanbul. Thus the 1953 hit by The Four Lads, "Istanbul (Not Constantinople)," which goes:

> Istanbul was Constantinople.
> Now it's Istanbul, not Constantinople.
> Been a long time gone, Constantinople.
> Now it's Turkish delight on a moonlit night.
>
> Every gal in Constantinople
> Lives in Istanbul, not Constantinople.
> So if you've a date in Constantinople
> She'll be waiting in Istanbul.
>
> Even old New York was once New Amsterdam.
> Why they changed it I can't say.
> People just liked it better that way.
> So take me back to Constantinople.
>
> No, you can't go back to Constantinople.
> Been a long time gone, Constantinople.
> Why did Constantinople get the works?
> That's nobody's business but the Turks.

Then we pass through various dynasties and partitions of empires until we come to:

AD 1449–1453: Constantine XI—The last Byzantine Emperor, indeed the last Roman Emperor, whose loss of Constantinople to Mehmet II in 1453 brought the whole shooting match to a close.

THANK JUPITER BOADICEA
LOST—ROME'S LEGACY
TO THE WESTERN WORLD

⊡⊡⊡⊡⊡

*P*lumbing, central heating, Scotland, Wales, Christianity, the layout of our major cities . . .

All of these things emerged in Britain thanks to the two invasions of Britain by Claudius (AD 43) and Julius Caesar (although strictly speaking, he had two goes, in 55 and 54 BC). And the other thing is Latin, of course. The invasions are why English is so full of Latinate words (around 65 percent of the total), why British schoolboys started learning Latin obsessively in the Middle Ages, why some of them are still learning it obsessively, and why this book is coming out.

The best writer about Roman Britain was the great historian Tacitus. His prose isn't easy, but it is certainly clear and a fine model. You can use the following passages either to test your Latin or just to get close to an eyewitness view of Roman Britain.

Tacitus wasn't actually ever in the country, but his father-in-law, Agricola, was governor of Britain.

In his account of the man, simply called *Agricola*, he describes Boadicea's revolt (or Boudicca, if you want to call her what she called herself, before later historians started playing around with her name).

When Claudius ordered the invasion of Britain in AD 43, the main target was Camulodunum (Colchester), the fortified Iron Age settlement of the Catuvellauni that had been ruled, until his death a few years before, by Cunobelinus (or Cymbeline, as in the Shakespeare play). Here is Tacitus in chapters 11 and 12 of the first book of his *Agricola*:

> 11. *Ceterum Britanniam qui mortales initio coluerint, indigenae an advecti, ut inter barbaros, parum compertum.*
>
> *Habitus corporum varii atque ex eo argumenta. Namque rutilae Caledoniam habitantium comae, magni artus Germanicam originem adseverant; Silurum colorati vultus, torti plerumque crines et posita contra Hispania Hiberos veteres traiecisse easque sedes occupasse fidem faciunt; proximi Gallis et similes sunt, seu durante originis vi, seu procurrentibus in diversa terris positio caeli corporibus habitum dedit.*
>
> *In universum tamen aestimanti Gallos vicinam insulam occupasse credibile est. Eorum sacra deprehendas ac superstitionum persuasiones; sermo haud multum diversus,*

in deposcendis periculis eadem audacia et, ubi advenere, in
detrectandis eadem formido. Plus tamen ferociae Britanni
praeferunt, ut quos nondum longa pax emollierit.

11. As is usually the case among barbarians, no
one's quite sure whether it was natives or foreigners
who first colonized Britain.

Because Britons vary so much in looks, you can
draw some conclusions. The Caledonians' red hair and
large limbs point to a German origin. As for the Sil-
ures in the west, their dark skins and usually curly
hair—and the fact that Spain is opposite them—
suggest that Iberians crossed the Channel a long time
ago and occupied the area. The Britons nearest to the
Gauls look like them; either because they share blood,
or because the climate in places so close to each other
has produced similar physical characteristics.

I think that the Gauls probably did invade this
nearby island. Their religious practices can be traced
to the British taste for superstition; their language is
much the same; both countries like facing up to danger and tackling it head on. Britons are more aggressive, though, as you'd expect in people who haven't
been softened by years of peace.

12. *Caelum crebris imbribus ac nebulis foedum; asper-*
itas frigorum abest.

Dierum spatia ultra nostri orbis mensuram; nox clara et
extrema Britanniae parte brevis, ut finem atque initium lucis

exiguo discrimine internoscas. Quod si nubes non officiant,
aspici per noctem solis fulgorem, nec occidere et exsurgere,
sed transire adfirmant.

12. The British sky is obscured by constant rain
and cloud, but it never gets really cold.

The days are longer than ours; the nights are clear
and in the extreme north so brief that there's barely a
dark moment between dusk and dawn. They say that,
as long as the clouds don't get in the way, you can see
the gleaming sun throughout the night; it doesn't set
or rise, but just crosses the sky.

The Roman occupation of Britain went well for a few
years until, in AD 61, the Britains revolted. Tacitus explains
why in chapters 15 and 16:

15. Namque absentia legati remoto metu Britanni ag-
itare inter se mala servitutis, conferre iniurias et interpre-
tando accendere: nihil profici patientia nisi ut graviora
tamquam ex facili tolerantibus imperentur.

15. After the Roman ruler left and they were no
longer scared, the Britons began to get worked up
about their servitude, to compare their sufferings and
exaggerate them.

"We only get treated worse by being long-
suffering," they said. "Much more is asked of people
who give way easily."

169

16. *His atque talibus in vicem instincti, Boudicca generis regii femina duce (neque enim sexum in imperiis discernunt) sumpsere universi bellum; ac sparsos per castella milites consectati, expugnatis praesidiis ipsam coloniam invasere ut sedem servitutis, nec ullum in barbaris [ingeniis] saevitiae genus omisit ira et victoria.*

16. The Britons got each other going with this sort of fighting talk and they declared war on us. They were led by Boadicea, a woman of royal blood—the Britons are indifferent to sex when it comes to royal succession. They attacked our troops, who were thinly scattered across our garrisons. They stormed our forts and they invaded our colony, which they thought of as the heart of their servitude. Burning with triumphant anger, the barbarians gave full rein to their savagery.

After the Romans suppressed Boadicea's rebellion, things calmed down in Britain. Tacitus wrote, in the following chapters, how the Romans went about recolonizing the country, not by force, but by culture—by getting the native British upper class to ape Romans by taking baths, eating banquets, and wearing the toga.

21. *Sequens hiems saluberrimis consiliis absumpta. Namque ut homines dispersi ac rudes eoque in bella faciles quieti et otio per voluptates adsuescerent, hortari privatim, adiuvare publice, ut templa fora domos exstruerent, laudando*

promptos, castigando segnis: ita honoris aemulatio pro neces-
sitate erat.

Iam vero principum filios liberalibus artibus erudire, et
ingenia Britannorum studiis Gallorum anteferre, ut qui modo
linguam Romanam abnuebant, eloquentiam concupiscerent.

Inde etiam habitus nostri honor et frequens toga; pau-
latimque discessum ad delenimenta vitiorum, porticus et
balinea et conviviorum elegantiam. Idque apud imperitos
humanitas vocabatur, cum pars servitutis esset.

21. The following winter we introduced measures
to calm things down. Agricola set up temples, markets,
and housing developments to ensure that these uppity
barbarians scattered across the country got used to a
quiet life of leisure and pleasure. He rewarded anyone
who was hardworking and laid into anyone who was
lazy. So people started to compete against each other
to behave well; they didn't have to be forced to be
good anymore.

Agricola also set up a liberal education system for
the sons of the gentry. He showed such a preference
for the inventive British over the dogged Gauls that
the British—who used to hate speaking Latin—fell in
love with the language.

They even fell for our fashions and started wearing togas. Little by little they were drawn to things
with a touch of sinfulness to them: drawing rooms,
hot baths, elegant dinner parties. In their stupidity

they called all this civilization, when it was all part of their servitude.

THIS AND THAT

The nice-sounding *hic, haec, hoc*—this and *ille, illa, illud*—are horribly irregular but pretty crucial. Say *hic, haec, hoc* very quickly and it develops a sort of pleasant poem of its own. Not true of *ille, illa, illud*.

	SINGULAR		
	Masc.	**Fem.**	**Neut.**
NOM.	*hic*	*haec*	*hoc*
ACC.	*hunc*	*hanc*	*hoc*
GEN.	*huius*	*huius*	*huius*
DAT.	*huic*	*huic*	*huic*
ABL.	*hoc*	*hac*	*hoc*

	PLURAL		
	Masc.	**Fem.**	**Neut.**
NOM.	*hi*	*hae*	*haec*
ACC.	*hos*	*has*	*haec*
GEN.	*horum*	*harum*	*horum*
DAT.	*his*	*his*	*his*
ABL.	*his*	*his*	*his*

	SINGULAR		
	Masc.	**Fem.**	**Neut.**
NOM.	*ille*	*illa*	*illud*
ACC.	*illum*	*illam*	*illud*
GEN.	*illius*	*illius*	*illius*
DAT.	*illi*	*illi*	*illi*
ABL.	*illo*	*illa*	*illo*

	PLURAL		
	Masc.	**Fem.**	**Neut.**
NOM.	*illi*	*illae*	*illa*
ACC.	*illos*	*illas*	*illa*
GEN.	*illorum*	*illarum*	*illorum*
DAT.	*illis*	*illis*	*illis*
ABL.	*illis*	*illis*	*illis*

While we're on the subject of fiddly little words that are pretty crucial, here is another one—*is, ea, id*—he, she, it, or that thing:

SINGULAR			
	Masc.	**Fem.**	**Neut.**
NOM.	*is*	*ea*	*id*
ACC.	*eum*	*eam*	*id*
GEN.	*eius*	*eius*	*eius*
DAT.	ei	ei	ei
ABL.	eo	ea	eo

PLURAL			
	Masc.	**Fem.**	**Neut.**
NOM.	ii/ei	eae	ea
ACC.	eos	eas	ea
GEN.	eorum	earum	eorum
DAT.	eis	eis	eis
ABL.	eis	eis	eis

THE SUBJUNCTIVE, I'M AFRAID

If anything is designed to make the blood freeze, the subjunctive is a quite brilliant fridge.

The subjunctive is the only thing in Latin that really is properly difficult and doesn't respond to the clinical logic that dictates most of its otherwise lovely neatness.

No one's quite sure what the subjunctive means in

English, and to make it even more complicated, it has all sorts of odd little uses in Latin. Best to think of the subjunctive first of all as the "let it be" word. Just on its own, with no warning, it usually has an obligatory force, i.e., "let the record state" or "let him go" would use a subjunctive.

A notable example is *Vivat regina* . . . —"Long live the queen," or, literally, "Let the queen live." Or *Caveat emptor*— "Let the buyer beware."

Then it's best to think of the subjunctive as the woulda/shoulda/coulda form; i.e., when there's a "would" or a "should" or a "could" around, it's a pretty good bet that you should use a subjunctive. Not always, but as a rule of thumb. (I fear I would lose you forever if I were to write out all the myriad bits of the subjunctive. Let me stick here to its definition and usage—for conjugation tables, Kennedy's your man.)

IF CLAUSES

So the subjunctive applies when you use "if"—that is, in a conditional clause, but only if there's an element of uncertainty signaled by woulda/shoulda/coulda.

"I'd love it if you would come to a little cocktail party I'm having for Hannibal Lecter."

That takes the subjunctive—because of the uncertainty in both the "I'd love it . . ." clause and the "if you would . . ." clause. If, however, there's no woulda/shoulda/coulda, and there's certainty in the conditional clause, you don't use the subjunctive. The sentence "If I go to the little cocktail party you're having for Hannibal Lecter, I will hide in the bathroom all evening" takes a normal verb because you will certainly hide in the bathroom if you take up the invitation.

"ORDERING SOMEONE ABOUT" SUBJUNCTIVES

As you'll know from above (*supra*), when you tell someone to do something directly—"Get off my land," "Go and see the headmaster and take the strangled stick insect with you"—that's an imperative.

But if you're then telling the story about how you told somebody off—"I told Prince Charles to get off my land," "Mr. Chips told Biggins to go and see the headmaster and take his strangled stick insect with him"—then you use the subjunctive.

The "to" in "I told Prince Charles to . . ." is translated by "*ut*."

Now, don't be put off by *ut*. It's a horrible-sounding word and is used to mean several different things, which is a bit daunting at first. But just translate it as "to" to begin with and you won't go too far wrong. Then, as you go through its different uses, you'll get better at handling it.

This use of the subjunctive is also called an indirect command.

CRUCIAL LITTLE WORDS

Y ou must know your prepositions and conjunctions, the little words that glue clauses and phrases together. Some consolation: they crop up so often that you'll soon pick them up in passing without having to learn them.

There are two groups of prepositions, those that take the accusative and those that take the ablative.

Prepositions that take the accusative

Ad—to, at

Adversus—against

Ante—before (easily remembered by gamblers—the ante is the bet that all poker players must lay *before* a hand is dealt)

Circa—about (abbreviated to c. in English: "I weigh c. a hundred and fifty pounds, give or take fifty pounds")

Circum—around (thus circumference, circumnavigate, etc.)

Extra—outside, without (this has confusingly mutated into meaning more of something; its original meaning is better seen in words like extradite, meaning "to place outside")

Infra—below (used in footnotes in English books)

Inter—between (thus intercourse, interfere, interpolate)

Intra—within (a precise, useful distinction from *inter*; thus *"Eum inter cordem iecurque confodi"*—"I stabbed him between the heart and the liver"—and *"Eum intra cordem confodi"*—"I stabbed him in the heart")

Iuxta—next to (thus juxtapose)

Ob—because of (easily remembered by switching *ob* around, to get b.o., because of)

Per—through (thus perambulate, peradventure)

Post—after (thus post mortem, posterior)

Prope—near

Propter—because of

Supra—above (again used in footnotes in English books)

Trans—across (thus the Trans-Siberian Express, transfer, transvestite—literally across-clothes, from *trans* and *vestis, is* f.—clothes)

Ultra—beyond (mutated now in English to mean bloody huge, but still recognizable in its old form in words like ultra-montane authority—the power exercised by popes beyond the mountains, i.e., on the northern side of the Alps)

VOCAB.

cor, cordis n.—heart

iecur, iecoris, n.—liver (considered the supposed seat of the passions by the Romans, especially of love and anger)

confodio, -ere, confodi, confossum—I stab

Prepositions that take the ablative

A, *ab*—by, with, from
Cum—with
De—about, concerning
Ex, e—from (thus extract, exude)
Prae—in front of
Pro—before, in front of (thus proclaim, proffer)
Sine—without
Sub—under (thus subterfuge, submarine)
Super—over (mutated to mean "above all else"; thus
    Superman)

There are also some confusing prepositions that take the
ablative when applied to something at rest and the accusative
when applied to movement toward:
    In—in, on (ablative); into, onto (accusative)

CONJUNCTIONS

These again are crucial and again crop up so often that they
gradually lodge in your mind. No need to learn them, then.

Et—and
-que—and (when tacked on to the end of a pair of
    nouns, *-que* joins them to mean "and": thus
    "Cheech Chongque")

Neque—nor

Etiam, quoque—also

Aut—either, or

Sed—but

Enim, nam—for

Ergo, igitur—therefore (*igitur* tends to be used at the
beginning of a sentence; *ergo*, like in English,
halfway through—"I fancied her, ergo I tried to
give the impression I couldn't care less about her."
Thus *Cogito ergo sum*, Descartes's axiom, "I think
therefore I am")

Tamen, autem—however

Tandem—at last (easily remembered: "'Tandem,' cried
the old man who had been waiting forever for a bi-
cycle that carried two people")

Ut—so that

Quod—because

Cum—since

Dum—while

Donec—until

Si—if

Postquam—after that

Modo, tantum—only

BEWARE THE IDES OF MARCH—ROMAN DATES, NUMBERS, WEIGHTS, AND MEASURES

The Roman way of doing dates was incredibly complicated and therefore provides a good example of the axiom—which I've just invented—that if something survived from Roman days, like pillars or words or central heating, then the Romans did it well; if something hasn't survived, like the Roman calendar, then they did it badly.

So we needn't really bother with Roman dates except for a few show-off points.

The Romans had several festival days in each month. The Kalends (incidentally one of the very few Latin words that begins with a "k") was on the first of the month. On the Kalends, interest was paid, and so it came to be called *tristes Kalendae*, "sad Kalends," that is, sad for debtors, marvelous for creditors.

The Nones tended to be on the fifth day of the month.

And the big one, the only one you need to remember, is the Ides, around about the middle of the month. For most purposes all you'll need to know is the Ides of March, which falls on the fifteenth.

"Beware the Ides of March," said a soothsayer to Julius Caesar, getting the date of his assassination at the hands of Brutus and Cassius in 44 BC spot on.

THE JOY OF SEX, AND OTHER ROMAN NUMERALS

Roman numerals are a rare exception to my axiom, *supra*—only the good things survive from ancient Rome. They are unwieldy and not nearly as neat as Arabic numerals, but they are useful for dates, monuments, and showing off. They are also very easy to learn.

Numbers 1–10 go:

I II III IV V VI VII VIII IX X

The important ones there are V—5 and X—10. If you want to do one less than these, you put a I in front; one more, and you put a I after. And this principle goes on all the way up through the other new letters:

So XX is 20. XIX is 19. XXI is 21.
C (for *centum*) is 100. XCIX is 99. CI is 101.

D is 500. L is 50. DL is 550. DLI is 551.

M is 1,000. And, if you want to go on adding 1,000s, you go on adding Ms. So the year 2000 is repre-sented by MM. The year 2007 is MMVII. And so on.

While we're on the subject, the numbers when written as words are very tricky in Latin because, like most words that are regularly used, they've become battered and irregular. One, two, and three are the only numbers that decline:

> *Unus*—one—is nice and straightforward, going *unus, una, unum,* like *dominus, mensa,* and *bellum,* with only the odd irregularity.
> *Duo*—two—is pretty odd, going *duo, duae, duo.*
> *Tres*—three—is completely unpredictable, going *tres, tres, tria.*

As with Roman numerals, once you have learned the written numbers from one to ten, you are pretty much there. From then on, they use combinations and permutations of those numbers. So:

> 1—*unus*
> 2—*duo*
> 3—*tres*
> 4—*quattuor*
> 5—*quinque*
> 6—*sex*
> 7—*septem*
> 8—*octo*

9—*novem*

10—*decem*

11—*undecim* (i.e., combination of *unus* plus *decem*)

12—*duodecim* (*duo* plus *decem*)

13—*tredecim*

14—*quattuordecim*

15—*quindecim*

16—*sedecim*

17—*septendecim*

18—*duodeviginti* (i.e., two short of twenty)

19—*undeviginti* (one short of twenty)

20—*viginti*

21—*unus et viginti*

22—*duo et viginti*

28—*duodetriginta* (i.e., two short of thirty)

30—*triginta*

40—*quadraginta*

50—*quinquaginta*

60—*sexaginta*

70—*septuaginta*

80—*octaginta*

90—*nonaginta*

100—*centum*

200—*ducenti*

1,000—*mille*

With these few rules, a whole new world of tombstones and dates opens up. Epitaphs are always in very simple Latin, and the blast of smugness you get from being able to translate them, combined with the warm glow of remote mourning across many centuries, is pretty powerful, particularly if there's someone with you who's impressed by that sort of thing.

The best example is in St. Peter's, Rome, in the joint tombstone to the last three members of the Stuart family, kept from the throne by their Catholicism, their place taken by William and Mary.

James II's son, the Old Pretender, James Stuart, his son, Bonny Prince Charlie, and his nephew, Henry Stuart, who became a cardinal, are all buried in the crypt of St. Peter's, some way from the monument. The memorial is often littered with flowers, left by Jacobite romantics.

On the monolithic, white marble obelisk, with bas-relief portraits of the three men designed by the Roman sculptor Antonio Canova, the inscription treats James Stuart as if he had been king:

JACOBO III JACOBI II MAGNAE BRIT. REGIS FILIO
KAROLO EDUARDO ET HENRICO DECANO PATRUM CAR-
DINALIUM JACOBI III FILIIS REGIAE STIRPIS STUARDIA
POSTREMIS ANNO.MDCCCXIX

To James III, son of King James II of Great Britain, to Charles Edward and to Henry, Dean of the Cardinal Fathers, sons of James III, the last of the Royal House of Stuart. 1819.

Below the inscription are two weeping angels, symbolizing the lost hopes of the exiled Stuarts.

Opposite the monument to the royal Stuarts is a monument to Maria Klementyna Sobieska, wife of James Francis Edward Stuart and mother of Charles Edward Stuart and Henry Benedict Stuart. Its inscription reads:

> MARIA CLEMENTINA M. BRITANN. FRANC. ET HI-
> BERN. REGINA

Maria Clementina, Queen of Great Britain, France, and Ireland.

The reference to France is a relic of the Plantagenet claim to the French throne. Incidentally, a decade ago, when the Canova marble was beginning to look a little tarnished, an appeal went out among Jacobite supporters to clean it up. The chief contributor ended up being that secret Jacobite queen, the Queen Mother, who couldn't hide her roots stretching back to her birthplace, Glamis Castle in Forfar, Scotland.

TO YOU, PAL, THAT'LL BE TWENTY-THREE SESTERTII — ROMAN MONEY, WEIGHTS, AND MEASURES

Money

The most famous Roman coin was the *sestertius*, which literally means "two and a half" because there were two and a half

asses—the copper *as* was the basic unit of Roman currency—
to a *sestertius*, a silver coin.

The *quinarius*, also silver, was worth five asses or two *ses-*
tertii; the *denarius*, ten asses, or four *sestertii*.

Weights and Measures

The British Imperial and American measures are still
pretty much based on Roman measures with a few tiny differ-
ences over the intervening two millennia.

After the Romans left Britain, the Anglo-Saxons introduced their own measures—furlongs, yards, acres, pecks, and
bushels. And then, after the Norman conquest, the Normans
reintroduced Roman measures, resulting in a system that
mixed ancient Anglo-Saxon measures and Roman measures.

These units were standardized by the Magna Carta in 1215
and were periodically reviewed and updated (notably in 1496,
1588, and 1758). It was the UK Weights and Measures Act of
1824 that finalized British measurements as they stand today.

American measures were never cleared up in the same
way, and so they still have pre-Revolutionary measurements
like the King William bushel of 1696 and the Queen Anne
gallon of 1707.

As for those Roman measures, they were as follows:

The Roman *libra*, also called, confusingly, the *as* or a
pondo—thus our pound—was equal to about 12 ounces.
The *amphora*, as in an ancient two-handled clay

jug, was also a measure of liquid—a Roman cubic foot, equivalent to about seven gallons.

The Roman *pes* or foot, equivalent to about 11.6 inches, derived from the rough length of an adult male foot, is roughly the length of our modern foot measurement.

The longer unit, a *stade*, is equivalent to 625 Roman feet, or 607 imperial feet.

INDIRECT STATEMENTS

One of the most useful things about learning Latin is that it introduces you to the detailed study of grammar and syntax— something that is almost completely absent these days from the teaching of English.

So far, we've mostly looked at the different endings that Latin words have according to their role in the sentence. Now let's take a brief tour of just a few of the more common Latin constructions. We will start with indirect statements.

An indirect statement is when something that somebody said (or says, or might say, etc.) is being reported by the main sentence. So, suppose Aeneas says "Dido is miserable." We can report that statement in any number of ways:

Aeneas tells me that Dido is miserable.
I don't believe that Dido is miserable.
Surely it's no surprise that Dido is miserable.

Different languages have different ways of performing this important trick, although you'll also find that most languages have several different ways of doing it. English likes to use "that," and to repeat the original statement almost verbatim. In fact, we often even leave out the "that," which seems to make our method especially simple: Aeneas says Dido is miserable.

In Latin, the preferred construction looks like this:

Aeneas says Dido to be miserable.

Dido, in this case, becomes a quasi (*quasi*—sort of) object of the verb "to say" (and so goes into the accusative case) and the verb goes into the infinitive (retaining the tense of the original statement).

Aeneas dicit Didonem miseram esse.

I say Cicero has an incredible nose.
Dico Ciceronem nasum incredibilem habere.

He said Carthage had to be destroyed.
Dixit Carthaginem delendam esse.

I think it's time for a drink.
Credo nunc esse bibendum.

Caesar said he had come, seen, conquered.
Caesar dixit se venisse, vidisse, vicisse.

Princess Diana kept saying that MI6 were trying to kill her.

Diana, mulier regii generis, dictitabat homines sicarios et reginae servos se occidere velle.

In the last examples, the reporters of the statement (Caesar and Diana) themselves appear in the reported statement. So it comes out like this: "Caesar said himself to have come, to have seen, to have conquered." "Diana kept saying assassins to be trying to kill herself." So you find a reflexive pronoun ("herself," "himself "): *se.*

Incidentally, this way of doing things might seem rather exotic, but it really isn't. It's fairly common in English as well: "I believe him to be innocent"; "I know it to be true"; "He considered himself to be one of us"; "I take all this to be obvious."

I WANT TO KISS A HOLLYWOOD A-LISTER

Simple desires just take the infinitive. So, "The stalker wants to kiss Cameron Diaz" is just *"Venator amatorius Cameronam Diaz osculari vult."*

Here you come across one of the nice pleasures of Latin—that it allows you to come up with new words for objects invented since Roman days, and to have a proper think about what the real meaning is behind a particular word.

The Romans didn't have stalkers—if you look at *The Rape of the Sabine Women* by Poussin, you'll see they didn't need to be halfhearted about these things. Shortly after the founding of Rome in 753 BC, the Romans found that there were many more men than women in the city, so they promptly invaded the next-door city, where the Sabines lived, and took all their women.

Given that the Romans had no need, and so no word, for something as furtive (*fur, furtis, m.*—a thief) as a stalker, we have to invent a word for it.

The expression I've used for a stalker is "*venator amatorius*"—"a loving hunter."

SCARED OF THE SUBJUNCTIVE

Fear clauses use "*ne* plus the subjunctive":

"I'm bloody terrified that my ex-wife will go back to her childhood sweetheart."

"*Timeo ne uxor ad amatorem pueritiae redeat.*"

VOCAB.

uxor, uxoris f.—wife

pueritia, -ae, f.—childhood

redeo, redire, redii, reditum—I return

timeo, -ere—I fear

amator, -ism.—lover

QUO VADIS, AND OTHER ROMAN QUESTIONS

When you're reporting that somebody asked somebody else a question, the verb in the question they ask goes in the subjunctive:

> Kitty Kelley asked Andrew Morton when Camilla traveled to Highgrove in the trunk of Charles's Aston Martin.

> *Kitta Kellea Andream Mortonum rogavit quando Camilla, in Caroli Astonis Martini tergo celata, in Altasilvam iter fecerit.*

VOCAB.
rogo, -are—I ask
Altasilva—Highgrove, literally "High wood"
tergum, -i, n.—back
iter facio—I make a journey.
celatus, -a. -um—hidden

While we're on the subject of questions, here are the main question words you'll need:

Quis, quis, quid—who, what. This is the interrogative pronoun, which is easily confused with the relative pronoun, *qui, quae, quod*, meaning who or which, as in "I know a man who does."

SINGULAR			
	Masc.	**Fem.**	**Neut.**
NOM.	*quis*	*quis*	*quid*
ACC.	*quem*	*quam*	*quid*
GEN.	*cuius*	*cuius*	*cuius*
DAT.	*cui*	*cui*	*cui*
ABL.	*quo*	*qua*	*quo*

PLURAL			
	Masc.	**Fem.**	**Neut.**
NOM.	*qui*	*quae*	*quae*
ACC.	*quos*	*quas*	*quae*
GEN.	*quorum*	*quarum*	*quorum*
DAT.	*quibus*	*quibus*	*quibus*
ABL.	*quibus*	*quibus*	*quibus*

Incidentally, it is from the interrogative pronoun that the ancient game of "Quis? Ego" derives. I say ancient because it has all but completely died out, except among Wankers. It was a simple game: a prep-school boy would hold a sticker of a famous soccer player up in the air and shout to the whole classroom, "Quis?" The first boy to answer "Ego" ("Me") got the sticker.

Quando—when. Familiar from the Englebert Humperdinck song of the same name: "Tell me when will you be mine, tell me, *quando, quando, quando*."
Ubi—where
Quam—how

Quantus—how big
Quotiens—how often
Qualis—of what kind
Qualis—of what type
Uter—which of two

All these direct question words take an indicative verb, i.e., the simplest kind, as we see below when Juvenal lists the questions put to him by a drunken thug on the street one evening:

"Unde venis?" exclamat. "Cuius aceto, cuius conche tumes? Quis tecum sectile porrum sutor et elixi vervecis labra comedit?"

"Where have you come from?" he shouted. "Whose stale wine and beans have you been stuffing yourself with? Which cobbler has been eating sliced leeks and boiled sheeps' lips with you?"
Juvenal, *Satires III, On Life in Rome*

VOCAB.
acetum, -i n.—vinegar
conchis, -is f.—bean
tumeo, -ere—I swell, am swollen
sectilis, -e—cut, sliced-up
porrus, -i m.—leek
sutor, -oris m.—cobbler
elixus, -a, -um—boiled

vervex, -ecis m.—sheep
labrum, -i n.—lip
comedo, -esse, -edi, -essum—I eat up

Things change slightly when you use "which" or "what" or, more often, "that" in the middle of a sentence, as opposed to in a question—i.e., "He loved the bus which went through Chelsea." Here you use the relative pronoun, *qui, quae, quod,* meaning "the one which" or "the one who": "*Currum amavit qui per Chelseam iit.*"

Currus, -us m. strictly means "chariot." Our word "bus" comes from a Latin-derived word, "omnibus," which wasn't actually used by the Romans. It comes from the dative plural of *omnis, -is, -e,* meaning "all, every."

The name was coined by a wit, very possibly a Wanker, who, when asked what the big thing full of people was for, said, "It's 'for everyone'—i.e., it's an 'omnibus.'"

Anyway here is how you decline *qui, quae, quod.* It only varies from *quis, quis, quid* above in the nominative and accusative cases:

> NOM. *qui quae quod*
> ACC. *quem quam quod*

NUM AND NONNE QUESTIONS

You use *num* to introduce direct questions to which you expect the answer "no"; and *nonne* for questions to which you expect the answer "yes."

Matthew Norman put it well in the *Daily Telegraph* on October 3, 2005:

> Have you ever seen a match in which captaincy played a decisive part? (If you have, no letters please: that was what Latin teachers used to know as "a question requiring the answer 'No.'")

As opposed to:

> If Fergie's interviewed in *Hello!*, will she say something stupid?

> *Si Ferga in Ave! interrogabitur, nonne aliquid stultum dicet?*

> VOCAB.
> *ave*—hello, hail
> *miror, -ari*—I wonder
> *stultus, -a, -um adj.*—stupid

YOU HORRIBLE LITTLE MAN

Latin has a lovely way with diminutives, i.e., turning a normal thing into a smaller thing: as a rough rule of thumb you add *-ulus* on the end:

> "We've got this marvelous little man who comes in daily to massage my wife's head."

196

"Hunc homunculum mirabilem habemus, qui quotidie venit ut uxoris caput terat."

VOCAB.

quotidie—daily

caput, capitis n.—head

tero, terere, trivi, tritum—I rub

I'LL LOVE YOU SO MUCH THAT I'LL LEARN CONSECUTIVE CLAUSES FOR YOU

The above heading is a consecutive clause. Whenever you think something or someone is so lovely/horrible/odd-smelling that something happens as a consequence, use the subjunctive for the consequence, with the "that" translated by *ut*.

The failed writer hated Jemima so much that he drank all her wine at the party for her book, *Liberate Your Cellar Space*.

Scriptor incognitus Jemimam adeo oderat ut, cum in illo convivio adesset, in quo novum suum libellum ea recitabat, qui nomen habet Libera Cellam Tuam, *omne eius vinum ipse biberit.*

Or, more properly:

Iam res Romana adeo erat valida ut cuilibet finitimarum civitatum bello par esset.

Now Rome was so strong that, when it came to war, it was on a par with any of the neighboring states. Livy, *History of Rome I.IX*

VOCAB.

validus, -a, -um—strong
quilibet, quaelibet, quodlibet—anyone, anything
finitimus, -a, -um—neighboring
par, paris—equal
odi, odisse—I hate
convivium, -i, n.—party, feast (thus "convivial")
bibo, bibere, bibi, bibitum—I drink (thus "imbibe")

YOU LEARN FINAL CLAUSES IN ORDER TO BECOME ATTRACTIVE TO THE OPPOSITE SEX

Whenever you do something "in order to" do something else, Latin expresses that purpose by putting the verb into the subjunctive, and the "in order to" is translated by *ut*.

Again, "in order to" has a touch of Wanker's English, and is more usually encountered just as "to":

"Honestly, officer, I only drank the bottle of Calvados to calm my nerves after the crash."

"*Sincere, praefecte, Calvadi amphoram modo bibi ut
metus meos post magnum meum periculum sublevarem.*"

VOCAB.

destitutus, -a, -um—destitute
sincere, the adverb from *sincerus, -a, -um*—honest
praefectus, -i, m.—officer, prefect

YO, ROMANS—LATIN INTERJECTIONS

There are plenty of Latin words to suggest shock. But there
are only two you really need to know:

Eheu—"alas" (as in Horace's "Fogey's Lament"
from his *Odes*—*Eheu fugaces labuntur anni*—"Alas,
how the years slip by," see When in Rome, *infra*)

Ecce—"look," "lo and behold" (familiar to many
Latin prep-school veterans in the depressingly jocular
and second-rate exercise book, *Ecce Romani!*, its mock
laddish quality best translated as "Yo, Romans!")

GOLDEN LATIN—OR HOW TO
WRITE LIKE CICERO

𝄢𝄢𝄢𝄢𝄢

E ven though it's much better to dissolve compact, staccato Latin into chatty, free-flowing English, there are some lovely little Latin writing devices that, in both Latin and English, nicely loosen up the language. (You can tell, from their Greek names, that a lot of these flourishes were dreamed up by the Greeks and nicked by the Romans.)

Under Cicero in the first century BC, Latin hit top form, as the great Roman lawyer developed the figures of speech that still work today in written English, as well as in speeches.

There's a handy element of showing off in knowing all the names of these little devices—assonance, hendiadys, or whatever—but the key thing is to be able to use them. They are properly effective in English.

Alliteration—Use of consonants that have similar sounds.

Anacoluthon—Cutting short the first of two expressions to give the impression of haste or boredom: "I said that I would love her forever, that diamonds and roses . . . , but she went home with Brian."

Aposiopesis—When the obvious conclusion of a statement is left out.

> "The thing is, Deirdre, I think about you a lot, and I've never said this to a girl before, but . . ."
> "*Res est, Deirdre, de te cogito multum, et puellae hoc nunquam antea narravi, sed . . .*"

VOCAB.
de (plus ablative)—about
nunquam—never
narro, -are—to say

Apostrophe—Confusingly, as well as meaning ', apostrophe also means a statement, often a question, addressed to someone or something not present:

> "*Ubi est, mors, stimulus tuus?*"
> "Death, where is thy sting?"
> (1 Corinthians 15:55)

Assonance—Repeated use of vowels, to give a pleasing sound effect.

Asyndeton—The omission of conjunctions to produce a powerful combination of compression and flow, e.g., *Veni, vidi, vici*. This was a device much used by Churchill, however unenthusiastic he was about Latin at Harrow (cf. The Cases—Or Churchill's Problems with a Table, *supra*).

In his "We shall fight them on the beaches" speech on June 4, 1940, in the House of Commons, Churchill listed ten separate "We shall . . ." clauses before he used his first "and" as a conjunction between those clauses:

> "We shall go on to the end, we shall fight in France, we shall fight on the seas and oceans, we shall fight with growing confidence and growing strength in the air, we shall defend our island, whatever the cost may be, we shall fight on the beaches, we shall fight on the landing grounds, we shall fight in the fields and in the streets, we shall fight in the hills; we shall never surrender."

Asyndeton can get a bit tiring. Evelyn Waugh certainly thought so. It was exactly this sort of portentous pile of little Latinate clauses that made Waugh have the character Guy Crouchback, the protagonist in Men at Arms, call Churchill "a master of sham Augustan prose."

By Augustan prose, Waugh meant the so-called Golden Age of literature, which extended from 80 BC to AD 14, reaching a peak under the Emperor Augustus, with Virgil, Horace, Ovid, and Livy. Intricate and varied as those writers were in their poetry and prose, the neatness and precision of their

Latin meant that a "sham" version of it reduced it, in Waugh's eyes, to a series of simple, leaden platitudes.

Ellipsis—Ellipsis just means cutting words out, leaving them to be understood by the reader. The most common form of ellipsis is with the verb "to be," often left out for reasons of style and compactness. Say *"Paris Hilton bella,"* and a Roman will know you're saying Paris Hilton "is" beautiful. Ellipsis is also used of certain adjectives where the noun is so expected that it's understood, like *dextra, sinistra* (right, left), which understand the word *manus*—hand.

Incidentally, many dialects of English also leave out the verb "to be": in the African-American dialect, "She fine" or "You crazy"; in newspaper headlines, "Richard Burton dead"; in signage, "Exit at rear."

If you want to say whose mother or father somebody is, you don't need to include the words "son of" or "daughter of." So you would say, *Charles Elizabethae* (*filius* understood) or *Beatrice Fergianae* (*filia* understood).

Hendiadys—Using a noun as an adjective. So *"vi et armis"* literally means "with power and weapons," but the force of it is really "with powerful weapons."

This is a trick that isn't much good in English: if you want to use an adjective, use one; ditto nouns.

Hysteron-proteron—Putting the thing that happened second first for dramatic tension. The expression is from the

Greek for "later-earlier," and gave its name to the Hysteron-proteron club at Oxford, the one that liked to begin its meals with cigars and Calvados and finish with soup, breadsticks, and aperitifs. E.g.:

> *Moriamur et in media arma ruamus.*
> Let us die and rush into the thick of things.

> Virgil, *Aeneid* II. 353

Litotes—understatement. This often means using a negative to take the edge off a positive, as often employed by Anthony Powell, i.e., "not uninteresting" to mean "really quite interesting." E.g.:

> *Quaerite non sani pectoris auxilia.*
> Seek help for a mad [literally, "not sane"] heart.

> Propertius, *Elegies*, *Cynthia*

Metaphor and Simile—Exactly the same as in English but, once you think in classical terms, it's easier to remember that a metaphor (from the Greek, "to transfer") suggests that a day-to-day object actually is some extraordinary out-of-this-world other thing; while a simile (from *similis, -e*—similar) is *like* some other thing. So:

> *Caesar ab Italia volantem*
> *remis adurgens, accipiter velut*

mollis columbas aut leporem citus
venator in campis nivalis
Haemoniae.

Caesar rushed after Cleopatra as she flew over the sea from Italy, like [i.e., a simile] a hawk after soft doves or a hunter sprinting after a hare on the plains of snowy Thessaly.

Horace, *Odes* I: XXXVII, *The Fall of Cleopatra*

If Horace had left out the *velut*—like, this would have been a metaphor.

VOCAB.

volo, -are—I fly (as in Dean Martin's "Volare")

remus, -i m.—oar

adurgeo, -ere—I pursue closely

accipiter, -tris m.—a hawk

mollis, -e—soft (as in "mollify")

columba, -ae f.—dove (thus columbarium, a tomb with niches holding urns of ashes, like a dove-cote)

lepus, -oris m.—hare

citus, -a, -um—swift

venator, -oris m.—hunter

campus, -i m.—plain

nivalis, -e—snowy

Haemonia, -ae f.—the old name for Thessaly

Metonymia—The replacement by a dull word of one with more of a flourish, often with the name of its related god, i.e., referring to dance as Terpsichore, or war as Mars.

WARNING: This is a device often used by the camp and unfunny, by second-rate poets and the pompous and overweight, and must be used sparingly. The dangers are best caught in the Regency BBC series *Blackadder*, where Blackadder runs into Shelley and Byron at Mrs. Miggins's Coffee House, in ruffed shirts, loudly calling for "the juicings of the naughty bean."

A rather more classy example:

> *Quis post vina gravem militiam aut pauperiem crepat?*
> *Quis non te potius, Bacche pater, teque, decens Venus?*
> After wine, who bangs on about grave war or poverty?
> Who wouldn't prefer to talk about you, father Bacchus, or you, charming Venus?

Horace, *Odes 1.37, The Blessings and Dangers of Wine*

VOCAB.

crepo, -are, crepui, crepitum—chatter
potius—rather

Oxymoron—Putting together two apparent opposites (from the Greek for "sharp-stupid"), e.g.:

> *Tommasus Cruisus homo parvus magnus umbraculi est.*
> Tom Cruise is the little big man of the screen.

Paronomasia—Using similar-sounding words with different meanings.

> *Tibi parata sunt verba, huic verbera.* (Tacitus)
> For you words have been prepared; for this man, blows.

Periphrasis—The use of a long phrase when a short one would do—is not unlike metonymia, and is equally dangerous.

> *Nox caelum tundit, mox nobis castra ponenda.*
> Night bruises, and we shall be forced to camp.
> (Uncle Monty in *Withnail and I*, when it begins to get dark on the fells.)

Pleonasm—The use of pointless words, as in:

> *Humphreius Bogartus Laurenam Bacallam in labellis osculatus est.*
> Bogart kissed Bacall on the lips.

Polyptoton—Different cases of the same noun are dragged together.

> *Iam clipeus clipeis, umbone repellitur umbo; ense minax ensis, pede pes et cuspide cuspis.* (Statius)
> And now shield was repelled by shield, shield-boss by shield-boss, threatening sword by sword, foot by foot and spear point by spear point.

Incidentally, *cuspis, is m.*—spear point is where we get "cusp" from. Being on the cusp of something is often uncomfortable.

Prosopopeia—The personification of abstract qualities, also highly dangerous, and favored by poseurs. E.g.:

> O, *Iuventus, Iuventus, Iuventus dulcis; ubi es?*
> O Youth, Youth, sweet Youth; where are you?

VOCAB.

Iuventus, -utis, f.—the prime of youth, as well as the name of Italy's Turin-based soccer team (once you turn the I to a J, as the Italians often do—the Romans didn't use Js).

The name Juventus was coined by an appropriately young group of fourteen- to seventeen-year-olds from the D'Azeglio High School in Turin, who formed a team on November 1, 1897, using the black-and-white-striped shirts of Nottingham County Football Club to play in.

The Romans were nice and charitable about youth, and considered the prime of youth to last from the age of twenty to forty-five.

Synecdoche—Using the part of an object to describe the whole. We do it in British English—calling a car "a motor."

The Romans did it a lot: *caput* (head) for *homo* (man); *carina* (keel) for *navis* (boat).

While we're on the subject, we get our word "nave" from *navis*—from the ship-shaped (or, more confusingly, keel-shaped) wooden roof over the central spine of the church.

Tricolon—Listing things in threes, a real favorite of Cicero's. It's a trick taken up by comedians ("There was an Englishman, an Irishman, and a Scotsman . . .") and Hollywood scriptwriters (every episode of *Friends* and practically all other decent sitcoms have three separate plotlines).

Zeugma—Using a single verb or adjective in two different ways, e.g.:

> *Rem et eam manu accepit.*
> He took her point and took her by the hand.

WHEN IN ROME, TALK AS THE ROMANS TALK—A LATIN PHRASEBOOK

A few years ago, the English courts decided to do away with Latin because it was confusing some of their clients. Lawyers were up in arms, saying that there was no concise way of translating Latin expressions like *mutatis mutandis* ("after making the necessary changes"). Well, lawyers may have found Latin clearer than English. I doubt that their clients agreed.

All the same, there are a lot of Latin expressions that still survive and, while they're dying out, their use can still give you that I-know-this-and-you-don't glow.

Adeste fideles—"O come, all ye faithful!"

The hymn was originally in Latin, origin unknown.

Ad hoc—"For this purpose"

A genuinely useful word, meaning temporarily useful, i.e., "John Kerry was an ad hoc presidential candidate until someone more suitable cropped up, i.e., pretty much anyone."

"Wrapping up the showerhead with Scotch tape is a perfectly good ad hoc way of stopping it leaking, darling, till I can be bothered to go down to Wal-Mart for a new one."

Ad hominem/ad rem—"Dealing with an individual/dealing with an issue"

An *ad hominem* attack on Ronald Reagan's time as president would treat him as an individual, viz. John Hinckley, Jr., outside the Washington Hilton, March 30, 1981.

An *ad rem* attack would take the form of a *New York Times* op-ed by Maureen Dowd on the pitfalls of tax cuts and high military spending.

Ad infinitum—Indefinitely

Literally, "until infinite," memorably coined by Jonathan Swift:

> So, the naturalists observe, the flea,
> Hath smaller fleas that on him prey;
> And these have smaller still to bite 'em;
> And so proceed, ad infinitum.

Ad libitum—Off the cuff

Better known as ad lib, it literally means "at pleasure,"

but is most commonly used of the improvisation technique of the stand-up comedian, so there may not be much pleasure involved in the process.

Ad nauseam—Endlessly

Literally, "until sickness," used of things that go on and on: "As we entered the year 2020, the torrent of reality TV programs continued ad nauseam."

Advocatus diaboli—"Devil's advocate"

Also known as the *promotor fidei*, the "promoter of the faith," the devil's advocate is employed by the Vatican to argue against a beatification or canonization.

Also used of the willfully contrary, viz. Rush Limbaugh, Howard Stern.

Aegrotat—The malingerer's degree

Literally, "He is sick." This is the name for an unclassified degree given to a student who is too "ill" to do his exams.

Alea iacta est—"The die is cast"

Said by Caesar when, during his 49 BC battle with Pompey, he crossed the Rubicon, the river separating Cisalpine Gaul from Rome—the point at which he knew there was no going back, that war was inevitable.

Alias—Originally meant "at another time." Mutated to mean "also known as."

Alma mater—"Nourishing mother"
Used to mean your old university. The Romans used it to describe Ceres, goddess of agriculture, and Cybele, the nature goddess.

Alumnus—"Nursling, foster child"
The graduate of a particular university.

Amicus curiae—"A friend of the court"
Once used in law to mean a professional who isn't party to the litigation but is brought into court to give advice.

Anno Domini—"In the year of our Lord"
Abbreviated to AD.
When you write, say, AD 1987, the literal translation is "In the Lord's 1,987th year." This explains why there was never a year zero between 1 BC and AD 1. In this Christian dating system, modeled on years of emperors' reigns, you could hardly say, "In the Lord's noughth year" or "The noughth year of the reign of Nero."

Annuit coeptis—"He has favored our undertakings"
Taken from Virgil's *Aeneid,* this line is on the back of the great seal of the United States, and the back of the one-dollar bill. As is often the case, Latin is used to give a touch of class.

Ante meridiem—"Before noon"; thus a.m. and p.m., or *post meridiem*

Apologia pro vita sua—"A defense of his own life"

Apologia is in fact a Greek word, meaning defense, which has mutated into the word apology—although, for those who realize that the quickest way to get out of responsibility for something is to apologize without meaning it, it still is a sort of defense.

Apologia pro vita sua was the title of Cardinal Newman's autobiography (1864).

A posteriori—"From what comes after"

An *a posteriori* truth is something, derived from experience or investigation, that turned out to be true, or that we discover to be true by investigating the world: e.g., that human beings evolved from apes.

To be contrasted with an *a priori* argument—"from what comes before."

An *a priori* truth is one that is immediately obvious, without the need for any investigation of the outside world: e.g., that $2+2 = 4$, or that I cannot both be, and not be, in Rome.

A priori: Alcohol ruins the liver; Dean Martin drinks heavily; therefore he must have a bad liver.

A posteriori: Dean Martin has a bad liver; bad livers are usually caused by alcohol; therefore Martin probably drinks heavily.

Arma virumque cano—"I sing of arms and the man"

The first line of the *Aeneid*. *Arms and the Man* is also the title of a George Bernard Shaw comedy (1894). It is also the only line that most classicists can remember, and therefore the only line that bluffers need remember.

Ars longa, vita brevis—"Art is long, but life is short"

This is the Latin version of a saying thought up by Hippocrates (as in the Hippocratic Oath). Hippocrates meant that the amount that a doctor needs to figure out is vast, and life is short—i.e., too short to figure it all out. This was a recognition of the limitations of our knowledge and abilities, typical of the intellectual humility of the Greek enlightenment. What he was saying was, "Life is short, mastering the art is long."

The saying has now changed its force to mean that artistic creations live on long after the death of their creators.

The expression is a good example of the Latin phobia of the verb "to be." Quite often it's left out altogether, to make things sound neat and trim.

Aura popularis—Fleeting fame

This literally means the "popular breeze," used by Cicero of anybody who is the people's favorite for a while.

Aura has mutated into meaning a sort of mystical charm that lasts slightly longer than the average wind blows for.

Ave atque vale—"Hail and farewell"

Said by Catullus on his brother's death:

"*Atque in perpetuum, frater, ave atque vale.*"
"Hello and good-bye forever, brother."

Could also be used by the sufficiently confident/pompous on bumping into somebody in the street you don't want to talk to very much.

Ave Maria—"Hail Mary"
The angel's annunciation to the Virgin, telling her of impending motherhood, from Saint Luke's Gospel. The full text is:

> *Ave Maria, gratia plena, Dominus tecum. Benedicta tu in mulieribus, et benedictus fructus ventris tui, Iesus. Sancta Maria, Mater Dei, ora pro nobis peccatoribus, nunc, et in hora mortis nostrae. Amen.*
>
> Hail Mary, full of grace. The Lord is with thee. Blessed art thou amongst women, and blessed is the fruit of thy womb, Jesus. Holy Mary, Mother of God, pray for us sinners, now and at the hour of our death. Amen.

Benedictus benedicat—"May the blessed one give a blessing"
The shortest form of grace before eating.
Say under breath, just loud enough to be heard by your neighbor at dinner if you want to give off an accidental impression of holiness and private education.

Bona fide—"In good faith"
Used of transactions that often end up going wrong but were meant with the best of intentions. Bona fide is in the ablative.

The nominative works, too—when Eddie Murphy picked up a transsexual prostitute, it was a *bona fides* transaction on his part, since he believed he was paying the going rate for a pretty woman. It was a *mala fides* (bad faith) transaction on hers/his. Well, that's if you believe that Eddie Murphy's press statement was bona fide.

Carpe diem—"Seize the day"
From Horace's *Odes*,

> *Dum loquimur, fugerit invida Aetas:*
> *carpe diem, quam minimum credula postero.*
> As long as we're talking, hostile time is fleeing: so get a bloody move on, instead of hanging around hoping for something better to turn up.

And from P. G. Wodehouse's *Much Obliged, Jeeves:*

> "Carpe diem, the Roman poet Horace advised. The English poet Herrick observed the same sentiment when he suggested that we should gather rosebuds while we may. Your elbow is in the butter, sir."

Casus belli—The justification for making war
Much employed at the opening of the war in Iraq in 2003, but in use for centuries before. Thomas Aquinas wrote extensively about the circumstances in which war, particularly a holy war, was justified.

Caveat—Warning

Literally, "let him beware," *caveat* is used as a warning when you should be aware of the exception to the rule. E.g., "The Adelaide beaches are long, sandy, and sun-kissed. There is a caveat—Great Whites like them, too."

Caveat emptor—"Let the buyer beware"

The shopkeeper's cry and, for a long time, the traditional position in law: it was up to the purchaser to make sure he was getting what he wanted before buying it. After that, he had no redress.

More and more, with the rise of the guarantee and the growth of consumer protection law, it's more like *Caveat venditor*—"Let the seller beware."

Cave canem—"Beware of the dog"

Sign outside Roman suburban villas. The original mosaic is in Pompeii, the gentrified Brooklyn of Italy (*supra*).

Cf—Look

Originally an abbreviation for confer, which in Latin meant "compare."

Used to mean, "Look elsewhere in this list I've given you." So, in *The Rock and Roll Dictionary*:

O'Sullivan, Gilbert—*cf.* "Stars, Washed-up 70s."

Codex—A manuscript

Originally spelled *caudex*, it meant "tree trunk." Came to

be used to mean a book of wooden tablets, with words inscribed into a block of inlaid wax (not, as Asterix would have it, carved out of stone blocks).

Other useful book terms are:

Folio—edition, as in Shakespeare's first folio. From *folium*—leaf, which mutated into *folium*—page.

Verso—the left-hand page in a book (from *folio verso*—"the page having been turned," meaning the first page you look at after turning).

Recto—the right-hand page, from *rectus, -a, -um*—not, annoyingly, meaning right-hand, but from *rego, regere, rexi, rectum*, meaning to guide or direct. So *recto folio* means "with the page set straight."

Coitus interruptus—Self-explanatory

From *coitus, -us m.*—a meeting. Can also mean "a coming together," but not always. Depends on participants.

Cornucopia—"The horn of plenty"

This crops up in a lot of Renaissance paintings, where some lucky virgin or similarly blessed figure carries round a horn the size of an old gramophone speaker, stuffed with flowers, fruits of the forest, and cornsheaves.

The idea comes from Amalthea, the goat that suckled the young Zeus. In return, the grateful Zeus gave the goat the power to produce whatever it wanted out of its horn.

Corpus iuris—"Body of law"

The collected laws of a country.

The expression used to have more weight abroad, particularly in France and its old colonies, like Louisiana, which depended on a body of codified law, called in fact Roman Law.

Britain and a body of law didn't originally go together. The British, like Americans, used to depend for their law on the slow buildup of case law or common law combined with the accumulation of government bills in statute law.

But the gradual incorporation of European Union statutes and conventions into British law means that more and more the British could be said to have a *corpus iuris*.

Cum laude—"With praise"

Much more widely recognized in America, where the expression *magna cum laude*—"with great praise" is used of the second best degrees. *Summa cum laude*, "with greatest praise," is used of the best, while the not very good students are informally awarded degrees *summa cum difficultate*—"with the greatest difficulty."

Curriculum vitae—A CV or résumé

This literally means "the course of your life," which shows what careerists the Romans are; that the sum total of your existence is reduced to what you got in your SATs, whether you were a team player during your holiday job in the local Walgreens, and how quick your typing speed is.

De facto—In reality

A way of distinguishing from *de iure*—"according to the strict letter of the law." So: "The *de iure* Prince of Wales is Prince Charles. The *de facto* Prince of Wales is Tom Jones."

De gustibus non est disputandum—"There is no disputing about tastes"

A rare use of the gerund, literally meaning, "It is not to be disputed about tastes."

If you want to show off and imply that this is the sort of expression you use the whole time, even if nobody else does, it's enough to say, "*De gustibus . . .* ," and leave the rest of the expression hanging in the air:

"There's no question about it. Meatloaf and Michael Bolton rule."

"*De gustibus . . .*"

Dei gratia—"By the grace of God"

Delenda est Carthago—"Carthage must be destroyed"

Said by Cato during the Third Punic War (149–146 BC), after several centuries of Carthage being public enemy number one. Good sort of expression to be used by those who want to seem powerful in a world-weary way and are finally exerting the power they've always had: "Look—we've been to your mother's for New Year's Eve for thirty-seven years in a row. I've just got to go to the Lakers game this year. *Delenda est Carthago.*"

Delirium tremens—"Trembling delirium"

Used of the hallucinations and shakes of heavy drinkers. Often abbreviated to "the DTs."

De mortuis nihil nisi bonum—"Speak nothing but good about the dead"

One of the great lies: see behavior of Romanian peasantry on the death of Nicolae Ceausescu, 1989; uncontained joy in London on the suicide of Adolf Hitler, 1945.

Deo volente—"God willing"

Often abbreviated to D.V. "Hillary Clinton won't try to make a joke in her next campaign speech, D.V."

De profundis—"From the depths"

Usually of despair. Taken from Psalm 130—"Out of the depths have I cried unto thee, O Lord."

Also the title of the letter written in prison by Oscar Wilde to the man who'd got him there in the first place: his lover, Lord Alfred Douglas.

Deus ex machina—"A god out of the machine"

The fallback of the desperate writer who suddenly wants to tie up the end of a story with the extraordinarily unlikely appearance of somebody who explains the whole plot:

> "Clearly, Watson, it must have been Professor Wormbridge that did it. He's just published a paper in the *New Scientist*, explaining how he's the only man

on earth who knows how to make a new form of strychnine out of Oxford University's house ink."

"That's a bit of a *deus ex machina*, isn't it, Holmes?"

From the practice of lazy ancient Greek dramatists who liked to land a God on stage with a mechanical crane at the end of their plays to explain everything.

Domine, dirige nos—"Lord, guide us"
The motto of the City of London.

Dramatis personae—"The persons of the drama"
The cast of a play.

Ecce homo—"There's the man"
The words spoken by Pontius Pilate (John 19.5) as he pointed to Jesus in his crown of thorns.

e.g., exempli gratia—"For the sake of example"
Should be used only to introduce an example, not, like i.e., *id est*, "that is," to expand on and explain what you're talking about.

Eheu fugaces labuntur anni—"Alas, how the years slip by"
From Horace's *Odes*. Can be neatly shortened to *Eheu fugaces*, whenever you see something that makes you feel old: policemen getting younger; your friends appearing in obituaries; your first intimations that nightclubs are not really that enjoyable.

Emeritus—Honorary, well-earned

An emeritus professor won't do a full professor's job but is given the title as a reward for long service.

Ergo—"Therefore"

As in: "The junior head of accounts in Lillysmith's Paints was deeply disgusting to secretaries and odiously sycophantic to his bosses; ergo he got promoted."

Seems a bit pompous because you might as well say "therefore" instead of ergo. But it has a nice axiomatic quality to it, implying that this is always the way with junior heads of accounts, secretaries, and bosses.

Erratum—"Mistake"

The errata slip in a book will list as many mistakes as the publisher has found after the proof has gone to the printers.

Et al.—"And the other people"

Short for *et alii*.

Etc.—Abbreviation for *et cetera*, meaning "and the other things" (N.B. two words; Wankers might want to pronounce them as such.)

Et in Arcadia ego—"And I, too, have lived in Arcadia"

Arcadia, in the Greek Peloponnese, was a blissful rural idyll. This inscription is found on a tombstone in a Poussin picture. It's also a chapter heading in *Brideshead Revisited*, the one where Charles Ryder has a good time at Oxford.

Et tu, Brute—"You too, Brutus?"

Brutus is in the vocative here and should also be in deep disgrace for turning on his old friend Caesar.

Can be used of any once loyal friend. "Et tu, Divine Brown?" (Hugh Grant, June 1995).

Awkwardly, from the point of view of this book singing the praises of Latin, Caesar actually spoke to Brutus in Greek, and said something slightly different: *Kai su, teknon?*"—"You too, my child?"

Ex cathedra—"With authority."

Literally, "from the chair."

When a pope speaks *ex cathedra*, he is speaking in his official capacity, and ergo infallibly. Can be used in other contexts:

> "Roger Federer should be shot for that fumbled lob."
>
> John McEnroe was not speaking *ex cathedra* when he made that remark on ABC last night.

Exeat—Holiday

Literally, "let him be absent," *exeat* was first used for priests allowed out of the monastery for a few days. Later used for schools and universities.

Exeunt/Exit—The characters or character walk/s off stage.

A useful stage direction.

Ex libris—From the library of . . .
Literally, "from the books of." Usually found on bookplates.

Ex officio—"By virtue of office"
An entitlement to some job or another by virtue of your grand standing in some other job. So: "Because she was the Queen, she was *ex officio* chief of the Clan McTavish with special proprietary duties for the upkeep of the Western Stromness lighthouse."

Ex post facto—"After the fact"
E.g., "The NBC studio was full of *ex post facto* experts on September 1, 1997, saying it was mad to drive through Parisian underpasses at 160 m.p.h. with a drunk chauffeur at the wheel."

Ex tempore—Off the cuff
Literally, "of the time," often used as an adjective: an *ex tempore* speech.

Festina lente—"Hurry slowly"
I.e., if you want to get things done quickly, do them slowly.
Used by Suetonius of Augustus, who very slowly turned Rome from a republic to an empire, with none of the rebellions that might have happened if he'd done it quickly.

Fidus Achates—Loyal friend
Used by Aeneas of his best friend, "faithful Achates,"

who was always doing his best to cheer up his boss when the job of founding Rome was looking like an uphill task.

Floruit—Golden period

Literally, "he flourished" from *floreo, -ere, -ui*—bloom, flower.

Used particularly of artists and writers, and often as an abbreviation (Evelyn Waugh, fl. 1925–60; John Holmes, fl. 1970–4).

Fons et origo—The original source

Literally, "the fountain and origin." Used particularly of pioneers: "Hugh Hefner was the *fons et origo* of the porn industry."

Habeas corpus—A protection against arbitrary imprisonment

Literally, "you must have the body" (from the present subjunctive of *habeo: habeam, habeas, habeat* . . .). The "*habeas corpus*" writ is a cornerstone of British and American law. It means that any person must be brought before a court—i.e., "you must have the body" in court—and have his case investigated before he's put in jail.

Ibid.—"In the same place," short for *ibidem*

Very useful when compiling lists or anything where a long expression is repeated, particularly, say, in the explanation of the location of footnotes at the end of a scholarly book:

Chapter 7

1. *Sexing Shakespearean Hermeneutics and the Other,* page 27.

2. ibid., page 31.

Can be used in other contexts: "On May 1, I found Peter O'Toole in the Plasterers' Arms, sitting next to a table covered with empty glasses of Chablis spritzers. On May 2, I bumped into Peter O'Toole (ibid.). Three years later, I ran into Peter O'Toole (ibid.)."

In flagrante delicto—Caught red-handed
Literally "in the middle of a burning crime." Used of crooks and surprised lovers.

Infra dignitatem—"Beneath your dignity"
Shortened to *infra dig.* to mean naff or rude, below the belt.
"All I did was say your Honda Civic sedan was no Maserati. Punching my teeth out was a bit *infra dig.*"

In loco parentis—"In the place of a parent"
E.g., "We've been using the Cartoon Network *in loco parentis* for twenty years and Nigel seems perfectly well adjusted."

In medias res—Straight to the meat of it
Literally, "in the middle of things," used of arriving suddenly in the thick of it:
"George Bush was sworn in as president in January 2001, and found himself *in medias res* eight months later."

In memoriam—"In memory of "

In nomine Patris et Filii et Spiritus Sancti—"In the name of the father, the son, and the Holy Ghost"

Inter alia—"Among other things"

E.g.: "The pub bore in the Albion touched on, *inter alia*, how MI6 had killed Princess Diana and the fact that the druids had moved the bluestones of the Preseli Mountains by astral humming to Stonehenge."

In vino veritas—You tell the truth when you're drunk

Literally, "In wine, the truth."

In vitro—Artificial

Literally, "in glass," and so used of test-tube babies. As opposed to *in vivo*—taking place in a living organism.

Ipso facto—Because of that very thing

Literally, "by the fact itself."

"You work for the bank. The bank works for me.

Ipso facto, I'm your boss."

Ben Stiller, *Dodgeball* (2004)

The expression tends to be used of self-contradictory statements, where the fact of the statement being made itself contradicts the content:

If you have to explain how funny your joke was, then, *ipso facto*, it wasn't funny.

If you have to ask yourself if you love me, then, *ipso facto*, you don't.

Ius primae noctis—*Droit de seigneur*
Literally, "the right of the first night," the entitlement of a lord to go to bed with a serf's wife on her wedding night. It says much for English prudery that there is no English expression for this.

Lex Salica—"Salic Law"
The law of the Salian Franks, who lived in the north of modern Germany where the Rhine meets the North Sea. Salic Law is usually known for its refusal to let women inherit estates.

Litterae humaniores—Classics, the first two years of classics at Oxford
Literally, "more humane letters," *lit. hum.* as it is abbreviated to, covers the greatest hits of classics—poetry, prose, history, and philosophy.

The exam of the same name at Oxford was the longest exam in the world—thirteen three-hour papers in a week—before it was superseded by the Chinese Civil Service Exams (or so people like me, who've sat them, like to claim).

The Chinese Civil Service Exams have in fact been around for several thousand years. To begin with, they tested music, archery, horsemanship, arithmetic, writing, and knowledge of the rituals of public and private life. They later expanded to include military strategies, civil law, revenue and taxation, agriculture, and geography in addition to the Confucian Classics. By 1370, each sitting of the exams could be as long as seventy-two hours on the trot.

Locum tenens—A substitute

Literally, "holding a place," the expression is shortened to *locum*, for people with a temporary position, usually doctors or vicars. Note that the words shifted in French to *lieu-tenant*.

Magister Artium—"Master of Arts"

Abbreviated to MA—the degree one above a BA.

Magnificat—A song of praise

Literally, "it magnifies," from the Virgin Mary's response to the Annunciation:

> *Magnificat anima mea Dominum.*
> "My soul magnifies the Lord."

Magnum opus—A masterpiece

Literally, "a big work."

Mea culpa—My fault

Literally, "by my fault," being in the ablative. To add emphasis, say *"mea maxima culpa"*—my fault in spades.

Medicinae Doctor—"Doctor of Medicine"

Abbreviated to MD.

Memento mori—Remember that you must die

Literally "remember to die," used of an object that reminds you of your mortality—a skull, your fading grandfather, a ticking clock.

Mens sana in corpore sano—Healthy body, healthy mind

Literally, "healthy mind in healthy body," an idiom coined by Juvenal in his Satires, i.e., exercise is good for you.

Modus operandi—A way of working things out

Literally, "a way of working"—*operandi* is a gerund here (from *operor, -ari*—to work)—used normally of a compromise, a third way.

Modus vivendi—"A way of living"

Again, normally used of a compromise and, again, *vivendi* is a gerund here (from *vivo, vivere*—to live). So, "I was keen on watching *Wife Swap*. She preferred listening to Bach. So we established a *modus vivendi*, where we agreed never to be in the drawing room at the same time."

Ne plus ultra—The best

Literally, the "no more further," it tends to be used of things that are far and away the best in their field, no contest.

"Jon Stewart is the *ne plus ultra* of satirical television."

Nil desperandum—Don't worry

Literally, "nothing is to be despaired about." The "is" is

understood. *Desperandum* is a gerundive. The expression was used in Horace's *Odes*.

Non omnis moriar—"I shall not altogether die"
Used in Horace's *Odes* to declare that his works would live on after him.

Non sequitur—An illogicality
Literally, "it doesn't follow."

"His name," said Flick, "is Roderick Pyke. That's why I'm running away."
This struck Bill as a *non sequitur*. Women do eccentric things, but surely the most temperamental girl would hardly leave her home simply because a man's name was Roderick Pyke.
P. G. Wodehouse, *Bill the Conqueror* (1924)

Novus ordo seclorum—"A new order of the ages"
This motto is printed on the back of the dollar bill, with the implication that a new order was born on the invention of the United States. While we're on the subject, America's motto is *e pluribus unum*—one out of many, i.e., America was formed out of lots of separate states.

Nunc dimittis—"Now you may leave"
Taken from *Nunc dimittis servum tuum, Domine*—"Now you send your servant away, Lord." (St. Luke).
Used of any official permission to leave.

Money shot

Obiit—"He died"

Abbreviated to ob. in people's dates (Babe Ruth, fl. 1914–35, ob. 1948). See "*floruit*"—*supra*.

Obiit sine prole—"Died without issue"

Abbreviated to o.s.p. in genealogy reference books.

Oderint dum metuant—"Let them hate, as long as they fear"

The motto of the boss from hell, and the Emperor Caligula.

Odi et amo—"I hate and love"
Catullus sums up intense passion.

Pace—Respectfully disagreeing with
Literally means "at peace," though that doesn't help very much, e.g., "*Pace* Prince Charles, organic food can be disgusting and modern buildings can be okay."

Pari passu—"At the same pace"
Used to describe two enterprises being treated in the same way, e.g., "We've been using the construction of the Freedom Tower as a template for our builders. *Pari passu*, we should have unclogged the sink by 2025."

Passim—"Everywhere"
Used in particular of literary works.
"The tendency for novelists to start using familiar words for new meanings, like 'sock' for flat and 'rug rethink' for haircut (Martin Amis, *passim*), is a relatively new phenomenon."

Paterfamilias—Patriarch
Literally, "the father of the family."

Pax Romana/Americana—"Roman/American peace"
Used to describe peace imposed on a grand scale. Often used now of Pax Syriaca—Peace in Syria.

Pecunia non olet—"Money doesn't smell"

The rallying cry of financiers worldwide, viz. Butch Cassidy, Jack Abramoff, Sundance Kid, etc.

Per ardua ad astra—"Through perils to the stars"

The motto of the British Royal Air Force.

Per capita—Individually

Literally, "by the heads."

Per impossibile—Hypothetically

Another useful expression confined to Latin that doesn't quite transfer to English. It means, "assume the impossible."

"Imagine, *per impossibile*, that you were faithful to your girlfriend, Mr. Hefner, and that you were offered a million dollars to sleep with another woman."

Per se—In and of itself

Literally, "through itself," the expression is used to denote some hidden aspect of an object.

This is how the restaurant, Per Se, overlooking Central Park in New York, one of only four restaurants in the city with three Michelin stars, got its name. Its chef, Thomas Keller, available to cater private parties at $300,000 a throw, was asked if his new, as yet unnamed restaurant, would be similar to his California restaurant, the French Laundry. "It won't be the same, per se," Keller said. And the name stuck.

Persona non grata—"An unacceptable person"

Because we're more interested in stories about gate-crashers than life-enhancers, *persona non grata* is used much more often than the expression it grew out of, *persona grata*.

Post mortem—"After death"

An autopsy.

Post partum—"After birth"

From *partus, -us, m.*—a birth.

Post scriptum—"After having been written"

As in P.S., from the past participle of *scribo, scribere, scripsi, scriptum*—I write.

Prima facie—"At first appearance"

Primus inter pares—"First among equals"

Used when somebody is chosen as the leader of a group of equally qualified people. The leader may have extra powers allotted to him in order to carry out his duties, but he is in no way considered superior to his contemporaries.

Pro bono publico—"For the public good"

The fuller version of *pro bono*, as in *pro bono* lawyers who do work for free.

Pro forma—For form's sake

Literally, "for form," *pro forma* is now most regularly used of an invoice sent to a buyer in advance of the ordered goods.

Pro rata—"In proportion"

Qua—"In the capacity of "

Derived from the ablative feminine singular of *qui*—who or what.

> "Dr. Murgatroyd was most encouraging. He said the spots qua spots . . . Is it qua?"
> "Perfectly correct, sir."

> Bertie Wooster and Jeeves in P. G. Wodehouse's
> *Aunts Aren't Gentlemen* (1974)

QED, quod erat demonstrandum—"The thing that was to be proved"

This expression was originally used in math problems. You would be given some equation, say, $e=mc^2$, and then once you'd proved it, you'd write QED at the end. Then the expression came to be used in arguments:

"Paul McCartney is a genius."

"No, he's not."

"What about the Beatles?"

"Listen to that frog song. Or anything by Wings. QED."

Quid pro quo—Something for something

Literally "What for what?"

E.g., "If I come to the James Blunt concert with you, there's got to be a *quid pro quo*—am I allowed not to go shopping with you tomorrow?"

Quis custodiet ipsos custodes?—"Who will guard the guards themselves?"

Juvenal, in his *Satires,* was referring to the problem of finding men to guard women suspected of infidelity while their husbands were out of town. Now the expression is more often used of people in powerful positions who then abuse that power.

"What can you do when a church leader turns immoral? *Quis custodiet ipsos custodes et Jimum Bakkerum?*"

Quondam—"Former"

Used as an adjective, but only by the pompous (cf. Wanker's Latin, Lord Patten of Barnes): "My *quondam* girlfriend flipped out when she saw me with her fat cousin."

Quos deus vult perdere prius dementat—"Those whom a god wishes to destroy, he first drives mad"

Derived from Euripides, this line was twisted by the English literary critic Cyril Connolly (1903–74) to "Those whom the gods wish to destroy, they first call promising."

He was referring not least to himself and the great burden of being thought brilliantly clever at Eton and being appointed a member of Pop, the school's society of the most popular boys; life was inevitably downhill from then on.

Quo vadis?—"Where are you going?"

Not just a bad 1951 film with Peter Ustinov as the Emperor Nero.

When St. Peter was fleeing martyrdom in Rome, he met Christ on the Appian Way going in the opposite direction:

> *Dicit ei Simon Petrus, "Domine, quo vadis?"*
> *"Quo ego vado non potes me modo sequi, sequeris autem postea."*

Simon Peter said, "Where are you going, Lord?"

"I'm going where you can't follow me now, but you will later [i.e., to martyrdom]."

John, 13:36

Rara avis—A rarity

Literally "a rare bird," from Juvenal's *Satires:*

> *Rara avis in terris nigroque simillima cycno.*

A rare bird in these lands and very similar to a black swan.

This was in the days when black swans were rare birds. The phrase has come to signify any sort of unlikely circumstance: "A bald American president? *Rara avis.*"

Re—Concerning

From *res, rei f.*—thing, matter, literally, "in the matter of."

Reductio ad absurdum—"Reduction to absurdity"

The principle, mathematical or otherwise, of taking a statement to its logical conclusion, which turns out to be impossible. E.g., "Being accused of rape doesn't matter in Hollywood. Just look at Fatty Arbuckle's career."

Res ipsa loquitur—"The thing speaks for itself."

Often used as an axiom in English courtrooms before Latin was banished from the legal system in the late 1990s. Quoted when a lawyer thought there was no need to prove something because it was so stark-staringly obvious.

"And where did the stain come from, Miss Lewinsky?"

"Well, here's the analysis back from the lab. *Res ipsa loquitur.*"

RIP, requiescat in pace—"May he rest in peace"

Nice use of the subjunctive.

Rus in urbe—"The country in town"

A corner of a city that is reminiscent of the country. "Oh, Marjorie, your deck in the backyard! Absolute *rus in urbe!*"

Can be used the other way round: *urbs in rure*—a little bit of the city in the country. "Boy, I got bored living in

Maine for a whole winter. I got cable installed. Pure *urbs in rure* bliss!"

Seq.—Abbreviation for *sequens* and *sequentes*, meaning "the following." Often used in notes for books, i.e., "cf. page 23 *et seq.*"

Sic—When put in brackets in a quote, "Wrong, but that was how the original speaker said or wrote it"

"No. That's how you spell 'potatoe' [sic]."

Dan Quayle, Munoz Rivera School, Trenton, New Jersey, 1992

When the Duchess of York received a letter from a journalist, referring to her incorrect use of a word, quoting her, with the word "[sic]" implanted, she angrily wrote back, "It's one thing to accuse me of getting something wrong; it's quite another to refer to my eating problems."

Sic transit gloria mundi—"Thus passes the glory of the world"

First written by Thomas à Kempis, in *De Imitatione Christi*, on the transitory nature of grand projects, it can be a useful show-off thing to say, ironically, at times of deep human shortcomings:

"Posh Spice made a lady? *Sic transit . . .*"

Silent leges enim inter arma—"Laws go quiet in wartime"

An axiom from Cicero's *Pro Milone*, often quoted by critics of George W. Bush when they write about Guantanamo Bay or the state bugging American citizens.

Si monumentum requiris, circumspice—"If you seek a monument, look around you"

The inscription on the tomb of Sir Christopher Wren in the crypt of St. Paul's, his masterpiece.

Often used in a heavy-handed way by journalists: "A-Rod. Si monumentum requiris, Yankee Stadium circumspice."

Sine die—Until an unspecified day

Literally, "without a day," a way of saying things aren't going to be resolved for some time. E.g., "After he had won the school math and computing prize, Nigel resolved to get a girlfriend *sine die*."

Sine qua non—A crucial condition

Literally, "without which not."

"The *sine qua non* of going to stay with your mother in New Jersey on Friday is that we leave by Saturday lunch and no later. And we're not having lunch."

Stet—"Let it stand"

An editor's mark by a crossed-out word or sentence that

243

he wants reinstated. From the third person singular subjunctive of *sto, stare, steti, statum*—I stand.

Sub iudice—Still before the courts

Literally, "under judgment," the words are a legal term, meaning that you can't say something prejudicial about somebody before their trial is concluded.

Sub poena—"Under punishment"

Much used in cop shows—"We'll slap a *subpoena* so fast on him, he'll think he's drowned in Latin"—the expression derives from English law, meaning a writ summoning someone to appear before court with a specified punishment if they do not appear.

Sui generis—A one-off

Literally, "of its own kind," this tends to be used not as a term of flattery, but as a precise way of denoting an oddity that doesn't fit the norm.

E.g., "When it comes to parking restrictions in Britain, London is *sui generis*."

Tabula rasa—A blank slate

Literally, "a writing tablet that has been scraped," used for an empty mind or a place without history.

Te deum—"A devotional hymn"

An abbreviated version of *Te deum laudamus*—"We

praise you, Lord." Also called the Ambrosian Hymn, because of its association with St. Ambrose (AD 340–397), a popular Bishop of Milan who was keen on the *Te deum.*

Tempus fugit—"Time flies"
The Wanker's twenty-fifth birthday wail.

Terra firma—Dry land
Literally, "firm land," popularly used by returning seafarers—"Great to be back on . . ."

Timeo Danaos et dona ferentes—There's no such thing as a free lunch
Literally, "I fear Greeks even when they're carrying presents." Said by the Trojan priest Laocoon when he first saw the wooden horse that brought the downfall of Troy.

Ultima Thule—The end of the world
Literally, "the end of Thule," from Virgil's *Georgics.* Thule was thought to be the northernmost island in the world, a six-day journey beyond Britain—the equivalent to going as far as Iceland.

Urbi et orbi—"To the city and the world"
The name for speeches made by the pope to Rome and the world.

Vade mecum—"Go with me"

Something you carry with you every day. It originally referred to a favorite book, but would now be applied to a Black-
Berry or bottled water.

Velis nolis—"Whether you like it or not"

The origin of willy-nilly. As in this sentence, where
Seneca is berating someone for not turning to Stoicism:

> *Tu occupatus es, vita festinat: mors interim aderit, cui*
> *velis nolis vacandum est.*
>
> You're busy, life is a rush: meanwhile death will be
> upon you, and you will have to make time for that,
> whether you like it or not.

Versus—"Against"

Abbreviated to v.

Confusingly, in British legal circles, you write Jarndyce v.
Jarndyce, but in order to put one over on nonlegal types, you
say, "Jarndyce and Jarndyce" (the case in Dickens's *Bleak
House*, which ran on and on for decades). A rare example of
lawyers choosing not to use Latin.

Via—"By way of"

The ablative of *via, -ae, f.*—way.

Vice versa—Conversely

Literally, "the change being turned."

Video meliora proboque, deteriora sequor—"I see better things and approve of them, and end up doing the worse thing"

Originally from Ovid's *Metamorphoses*, the cry of the recalcitrant drunk and the aspiring novelist.

Viva voce—An oral test

Literally, "with live voice," the idiom is often shortened to *viva* and is usually a test conducted after an exam to classify a grade when it is on the borderline between, say, a first-class degree and a second.

Martin Amis is one of the few Oxford undergraduates to receive a congratulatory *viva* for the outstanding first he got when he was at Exeter College. Summoned to the university's examination schools for a *viva*, he thought he was going to have to argue his right to a first over a second. Instead, the gathered dons stayed quiet and then burst into applause.

Viz.—Namely

Short for *videre licet*—"One may see."

"There have been some spectacularly successful good-looking politicians, viz. Ronald Reagan. But there have been many more failures, viz. John Kerry, Gary Hart."

Volenti non fit iniuria—"Injury can't be done to a willing person"

A legal concept that doesn't always hold true. In R v. Brown (1993), a group of British sadomasochists who had been happily nailing each other's testicles to the floor were convicted of actual bodily harm, after their defense of *volenti non fit iniuria* failed.

By the way, in British legal cases, the R, as in R v. Brown, stands for Regina—the Queen.

LATIN'S TENSE FUTURE—A
CONCLUSION

〖〗〖〗〖〗〖〗〖〗

Whatever you think of Mel Gibson's drinking habits and supposed anti-Semitism, at least he tried with his Latin when it came to his film *The Passion of the Christ* (2004).

There aren't many films with a credit for "Theological Consulting and Aramaic/Latin Translation," and Dr. William J. Fulco, the Jesuit priest brought in to sort out the locatives and the subjunctives, gets an alpha beta, if not quite an alpha, for his homework.

The Latin is pretty straightforward, and certainly pretty understandable by anybody who's gotten this far in this book.

"*Sanctus est,*" is Mrs. Pilate's view of Jesus. "*Facta non verba,*" is the Roman soldier's order to Christ, when he starts talking too much. *"Mortuus est,"* says Longinus, the soldier who sticks a spear in Jesus's side to check whether he's alive.

There's only one slip-up. If you are addressing a man from Judaea, you should use the vocative "Judaee," not "Judaeus," as was said in the film; *vide* Julian the Apostate converting to Jesus with his last, and grammatically correct, words, *"Vicisti, Galilaee"*—"You have won, O Galilean one."

Still, even Father Fulco's simple Latin will be beyond most schoolboys now. Latin in Britain and America is not quite yet a dead language. But it is dying. For all the supposed life that Harry Potter breathed back into the language, a negligible number of children are now learning it in any rigorous way.

Yes, they might be able to translate the Hogwarts motto—*"Draco dormiens numquam titillandus"* ("Never tickle a sleeping dragon"). But they won't be able to write a Latin poem in praise of Maggie Smith's acting skills or J. K. Rowling's philanthropy, or recite screeds of Virgil as any half-wit prep-school boy could half a century ago.

The number of grammar schools—high-quality free schools in Britain—has slumped in that time; and the number of children studying Latin in private schools and the remaining grammar schools has collapsed. In 1960, 60,000 children did Latin O level—the exam British sixteen-year-olds had to take until the mid-1980s. Now 10,000 do the much more basic replacement, GCSE (and, of these, in 2004, only 3,468 came from free schools).

When it comes to A levels—the exams taken by eighteen-year-olds in Britain—it's time to drag in the life-support machine: only 5,000 children a year take a classical A level of any sort; that's less than 0.8 percent of all A levels taken. And, if the future looks less than rosy for Latin, it's wine-dark for Greek. Fewer than a thousand children a year do GCSE Greek, squeezed out by its declining stablemate, Latin.

Of the three classical A levels (Latin, Greek, and classical civilization), it's easiest to score high marks for a correct translation in Latin. Yet the amount these few Latinists are expected to know about the mechanics of the language has withered away. Bye-bye to long summer afternoons spent in sweaty terror of chalk-stained bachelors slamming desk lids down on your fingertips if you don't know the gerund of *caedo* (*caedendum*) or the Latin for a funeral feast (*silicernium*).

How tragic it would be if the rigorous study of Latin were to disappear altogether in favor of more "useful" subjects. Because there is a need to learn Latin—if nothing else, to enlarge your appreciation of beauty, along the lines put forward by Robin Williams's character, speaking in favor of poetry in the film *Dead Poets' Society* (1989):

"We don't read and write poetry because it's cute. We read and write poetry because we are members of the human race. And the human race is filled with passion. Medicine, law, business, engineering, these are all noble pursuits, and necessary to sustain life. But poetry, beauty, romance, love, these are what we stay alive for. To quote from Whitman:

'O me, O life of the questions of these recur-
ring, of the endless trains of the faithless, of
cities filled with the foolish . . . What good amid
these, O me, O life?

'Answer: that you are here. That life exists,
and identity. That the powerful play goes on, and
you may contribute a verse.'"

So, learn Latin first for its verses and its beauty.

But learn it also for its language-teaching skills; in that
way it is a bit more like medicine, law, business, engineering,
and wiring a plug.

As Kingsley Amis has pointed out, it's wrong to think that
learning Latin is a sort of "mental gymnastics," a specially designed exercise for strengthening the mind. It's also wrong to
think that learning Latin will make your English better because
the two languages share so much. In fact, Latin is much more
precise and neater than English—and so you, as the translator,
have to make a conscious effort to jump from the register of one
language to that of another. Unlike most modern European languages, Latin and English aren't easily swappable, word for word.

As Richard Papen, the classicist narrator in *The Secret
History*, put it, "One's thought patterns become different when
forced into the confines of a rigid and familiar tongue. Certain
common ideas become inexpressible; other, previously un-
dreamt of ones spring to life, finding miraculous new articula-
tion. By necessity, I suppose, it is difficult for me to explain in
English exactly what I mean. I can only say that an *incendium*

is in its nature entirely different from the *feu* with which a Frenchman lights his cigarette."

The other important quality of Latin is the very quality that it is usually blasted for—its deadness. Because living languages are in a constant state of flux, there's a great deal of wriggle room when translating from one living language to another. Precisely because Latin is dead, there's none of that flexibility: this doesn't mean you can't be free and easy with your translations, but it does mean that you are much more likely to be definitely wrong in your translation if you haven't understood exactly what a particular word means or how a grammatical rule works.

So, there's not really much point in doing Latin unless you do it properly and learn it from its first principles. Which is why the drastic lowering of standards for exams like GCSEs is so depressing.

It's not all bad news. In America, which suffered a great slump in classics in the late twentieth century, there's a bit of a revival going on. In 1905, 56 percent of American high school students studied Latin. By 1977, a mere 6,000 pupils took the National Latin Exam. That zoomed up to 134,873 in 2005. But American Latinists have never been taught from the young age that British and European classicists used to be.

In *The Secret History*, Richard Papen gets some plus points when he turns up at the exclusive Hampden College in Vermont, and reveals that he's done two years' Greek at the age of eighteen—*but he's done no Latin*. When I arrived at Oxford to do classics at the same age, I'd done eight years of Latin and seven years of Greek. That tradition of learning classics from the age of ten or eleven is dying, as teachers and curriculum devisers take the age-old, defective answer to people refusing to do something difficult: make it easier, to the point where you squeeze out all the value that comes from a difficult exercise precisely because it is difficult.

The vice-chancellor of Oxford and the proctors are still rigorous about the conduct of examinations: "Rule (vi): Invigilators are strongly encouraged not to allow more than one person of each sex to go to the toilet at any time . . . Rule (xiv): Except for the drawing of diagrams, no candidate shall use pencil for the writing of an examination unless prior permission has been obtained from the proctors."

But when it comes to how much Greek or Latin you need, the vice-chancellor and his proctors are pussycats.

When I was practicing for my Greek A level in 1988, we translated chunks of the tricky Greek historian, Herodotus, out of 1950s O level papers. Now, to get into Oxford to read the alternative Classics degree, Mods B, you don't need any Greek at all. By the end of their second year, all classics undergraduates once had to know all twenty-four books of the *Iliad*. Now they can get away with just books one, nine, twenty-two, and twenty-four.

If you want to do a related classical subject, like Classical Archaeology and Ancient History, not only do you not need Greek; don't bother with Latin either.

It's going to get worse. Brilliant classicists don't become schoolmasters anymore. All the men who taught me Latin and

Greek at school, now in their fifties and sixties, had been Oxbridge scholars.

Of all my contemporaries who did Latin and Greek at school and Oxford, scholar or not, there isn't a single one teaching at a school. One taught for a while at the eminent London private school Dulwich College before switching to Philosophy. He still teaches a little Latin, but in an American college rather than an English school. That's typical. The teaching of even elementary Latin is draining out of schools and into universities—American universities in particular. That inevitably means that standards are dropping. Imagine what the state of mathematics or science would be if nobody started learning it until they were eighteen. Eventually, Latin will be about as well and as widely known as, say, Sanscrit, Aramaic, or ancient Egyptian—other languages that you can learn at university, but not at school.

Cicero had the right words for this desperate situation in the opening line of his attack on Catiline.

"How long will you abuse our patience, Catiline?" he said, in one of the first recorded rhetorical questions. "Oh, the times! Oh, the habits!" Or, as every schoolboy doesn't know, "*O tempora! O mores!*"

If you've read this book properly, however, you can become a 1950s schoolboy all over again and reach the sort of level where you can lean back deep into your armchair and bemoan how second-rate everybody else's Latin is.

To get your Latin going, it's worth buying Catullus's and Horace's poems. They're sometimes a bit tricky, so buy one of the Loeb translations. They have the English on one side and Latin on the other, and you can work your way through them pretty easily. Warning: the Loeb translations are a bit dreary and prim—in one translation of a juicy bit of Euripides, "sperm" is translated as "life whiteness." But if you can be bothered to keep two books propped open side by side, you couldn't do much better than look at Horace's *Odes* alongside a copy of the recent translation by James Michie, an accomplished poet in English.

And to brush up your Latin prose, get the Loeb of Caesar's *Gallic Wars*. Julius Caesar wrote in nice, clear, prep-school Latin, by the way.

To read the most famous Roman of them all, perhaps the greatest leader of all time, in his original language and to recite some of the most heartbreaking poetry ever written as it was meant to be read . . . Isn't that reason enough for learning Latin?

THE FINAL LATIN TEST

Here's the bit of Latin I set at the beginning of this book as a test for you to do—the epitaph on Leonardo Bruni's tomb:

> *Postquam Leonardus e vita migravit*
> *Historia luget; eloquentia muta est*
> *Ferturque musas tum Graecas tum*
> *Latinas lacrimas tenere non potuisse.*

I've printed the translation on the following page. If you can manage to translate it now, and you know what each verb and noun is doing in the sentence, congratulations—you have the basics. You can now eat as much pistachio ice cream and drink as many proseccos (or, as a Latin Wanker would put it, prosecci) as you want.

If you want to start looking at the Tintorettos, get a weightier book.

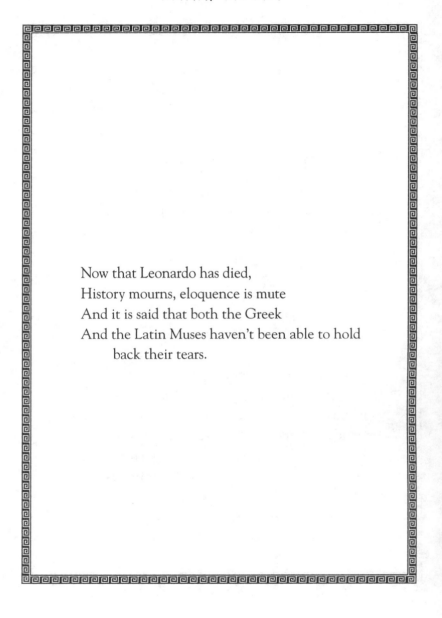

Now that Leonardo has died,
History mourns, eloquence is mute
And it is said that both the Greek
And the Latin Muses haven't been able to hold
back their tears.

ACKNOWLEDGMENTS

All at Short Books, especially Vanessa Webb, Aurea Carpenter, Rebecca Nicolson, and Emily Fox.

Alex Fox for his drawing.

My parents, Ferdy and Julia Mount, and my brother and sister, William and Mary Mount, for corrections and suggestions.

Dr. Adam Beresford of the University of Massachusetts for help *passim*.

Christopher Howse for advice on religious Latin.

Tony Ring, President, the International Wodehouse Association, for the use of Latin by Jeeves and Wooster.

The editor and publisher of *The Spectator* for permission to adapt *Return of the Dark Ages* (April 2004).

Stuart Conway for the author photograph.

The mistakes are all my own.

Harry Mount, Kentish Town, London
March 2007

259